MICROCOMPUTER APPLICATIONS IN QUALITATIVE RESEARCH

BRYAN PFAFFENBERGER
University of Virginia

Qualitative Research Methods,
Volume 14

SAGE PUBLICATIONS
The Publishers of Professional Social Science
Newbury Park   Beverly Hills   London   New Delhi

For information address:

SAGE Publications, Inc.
2111 West Hillcrest Drive
Newbury Park, California 91320

SAGE Publications Inc.  SAGE Publications Ltd.
275 South Beverly Drive   28 Banner Street
Beverly Hills   London EC1Y 8QE
California 90212   England

SAGE PUBLICATIONS India Pvt. Ltd.
M-32 Market
Greater Kailash I
New Delhi 110 048 India

Printed in the United States of America

Library of Congress Cataloging-in-Publication Data

Pfaffenberger, Bryan, 1949-
    Microcomputer applications in qualitative research / Bryan
Pfaffenberger.
        p. cm. — (Qualitative research methods ; v. 14)
        Bibliography: p.
        ISBN 0-8039-3119-0   ISBN 0-8039-3120-4 (pbk.)
        1. Social sciences—Research—Data processing. 2. Information
storage and retrieval systems—Social sciences. 3. Microcomputers.
I. Title. II. Series
H61.3.P43 1988
300′.28′5416—dc19   88-11554
                                    CIP

FIRST PRINTING 1988

When citing a University Paper, please use the proper form. Remember to cite the correct Sage University Paper series title and include the paper number. One of the following formats can be adapted (depending on the style manual used):

(1) KIRK, JEROME and MARC L. MILLER (1986) Reliability and Validity in Qualitative Research. Sage University Paper Series on Qualitative Research Methods, Vol. 1. Beverly Hills, CA: Sage.

or

(2) Kirk, J., & Miller, M. L. (1986). *Reliability and validity in qualitative research* (Sage University Paper Series on Qualitative Research Methods, Vol. 1). Beverly Hills, CA: Sage.

C O N T E N T S

Dedicated to Gerry Berreman

EDITORS' INTRODUCTION

In Volume 14 of the Qualitative Research Methods Series, Bryan Pfaffenberger has done much to clarify our options with respect to the role of computers in the thoughtways and practice of modern qualitative social research. They will not take on the burden, often thrust upon them by the atheoretical empiricists, of "thinking," or scientific reasoning, of data coding, analysis, or gathering. They will store data and work on command, and command is the problem. Computers are of course "good to think with," but they do not think. Like any other tool, they are embedded deeply in our assumptions, tacit and recognized, our various views of our arts and crafts, and always will be. Social structure and practice shape, define, constrain, represent and confer meaning on technology. How could it be otherwise?

This is not to obviate the debate over the precise effects that technology has on modes of thinking. The redolent idea, captured best perhaps in Ogburn's "culture lag" theory, that states that "culture" (whatever that means) lags behind "technology," is a simpleminded, unidirectional, commonsensible statement, not a theory at all. This idea has been dressed up in a new set of Emperor's clothes, now called "computer technology," and is said to shape not only work tasks, and "thinking," but sensibilities and politics. Much as the abacus, the potter's wheel, and the clock shaped earlier epochs, the computer is the new source of encodation for life. Such hypothecated deterministic theories should by now be summarily dismissed, but nature abhors a vacuum, and there is quite a lot of vacuous thought about. Where do the specific techniques computer programmers have devised fit with the broader, humanistic, and liberating goals of social science?

This book is rich with examples explicating the cultural context and therefore the limits of technological or even formal semantic definitions of meaning. The silent or invisible background assumptions of speech that must be brought to the speech, or action, must be brought to the coding or content analysis scheme, mechanical or not. Pfaffenberger brings such understandings not only to the cultural context of technological changes he uses as examples, but also to the context of computing as a code, as several physical operating systems, and as a tool. This sound and grounded knowledge saves the reader from trips to Heidegger's navel to gaze, the true-believer speeches of "born-again" technocrats, and the categorical bad-faith rejections of machines. This is a book from which one can learn.

—Peter K. Manning
John Van Maanen
Marc L. Miller

MICROCOMPUTER APPLICATIONS IN QUALITATIVE RESEARCH

Bryan Pfaffenberger
University of Virginia

1. INTRODUCTION

This book has two goals, first, to survey the many ways microcomputers and microcomputer programs can be used to further the goals of qualitative social research, and second, to do so *critically,* focusing on the potential liabilities as well as the benefits of using this technology for research purposes. Underlying every chapter is the conviction that microcomputer hardware and software can play a useful role in qualitative studies, but only if the limitations of the technology—and, especially, its potentially negative, or constraining impact—is kept in mind throughout. The text thus shifts between overviews of practical applications, critiques of the technology's limitations, and assessments of its potential impact on qualitative research. A passage extolling the merits of one type of software application, for instance, might well be followed by an exposé of the assumptions built into another.

This approach may strike readers as somewhat peculiar, particularly if they are accustomed—as people seem to be, for instance, when they read Marx—to adopt a stance that is either uncritically "for" or uncritically "against." Microcomputers, in particular, sometimes uncork a near messianic boosterism. In the opening, heady days of the home computer "revolution," for instance, otherwise sensible people argued that (as David Bunnell now recalls) small computers would "equalize opportunity for all races, creeds, minority groups, social classes—even help save endangered species" (Bunnell, 1987: 15). For others, micro-computers pose the threat of dehumanization, mechanization, quantification, and the sterilization of all that is warm and cuddly in human nature. To partisans of such extremes, I offer my apologies; my interest is to further the cause of qualitative research, and I am ready to take that which aids this cause and reject the rest. So this book is mindful, not only of potentially useful applications, but also of the potentially harmful impact of microcomputer technology in qualitative research.

Understanding a technology's impact is, however, itself a wonderfully complex matter, far more so than has been acknowledged until recently. When most people think about the "impact" of a technology, they have in mind the relationship of a *thing* (e.g., a material artifact, a machine) on people (e.g., the mind, social groups, patterns of social behavior, social values, and so on). Yet current directions of research in technology studies show convincingly that technologies—as Heidegger saw decades ago—are not fundamentally material. They are fundamentally social. Every technology is constructed in a social setting and a cultural environment. Woven into its material fabric are tacit social and cultural assumptions, such as a typification of the user, the social setting in which the technology will be used, the knowledge that the user will bring to the machine, and more (MacKenzie and Wajcman, 1985; Pacey, 1983; Pinch, Bijker, and Hughes, 1987). If we want to talk about the "impact" of microcomputer technology on qualitative research, then, we are obliged to talk about the complex relationship between the social dimension of this technology, a dimension of social thinking that is technically encoded, on the processes of qualitative research. The theoretical tools needed to analyze and grasp this complex relationship are only now being developed, and the efforts to examine them here will perforce be preliminary and speculative in nature. Yet it should become clear that the whole matter is in itself a fascinating and appropriate subject for qualitative inquiry. So this book, in surveying computer *methods* in qualitative research, also serves as an introduction to a *substantive* field, namely, the whole problematic matter of what happens when something inherently *social* lands right in the middle of social research. Such is the reason that the text speaks with two voices, the one practical and methodological, the other critical and theoretical.

It should be understood, too, that the aim here is *not* to provide a "how-to" guide to specific computers or programs. The approach is generic and conceptual. Specific programs come and go, after all, but software genres—such as, for instance, key-word-in-context concordance programs and text-oriented data base managers—remain remarkably stable—with, to be sure, occasional (but only occasional) accretions of some genuinely new phenomenon (such as expert systems). To put the point another way, from the perspective of sufficient distance (and detachment) one sees that the noisy hyperbole of the marketplace ("A revolution in data base management! An entirely new approach to word processing!") disguises the fact that the generic types of software have been around for some time, and will be around for some time in the future, in conception if not in fact. Much noise and messianic fervor is now attached, for instance, to the latest phenomenon of the computer avant-garde, hypertext, a textual data base that lets the user create associative trails of linkages among records. Yet such software was first envisioned by Vannevar Bush more than 40 years ago (Bush, 1945), and the concept has found its way repeatedly into information-management systems since that time. The idea that anything connected to computers is somehow unprecedented is itself one of the curious cultural phenomena associated with computing. The reality, often, is that the designers of computing systems carry into the computer world assumptions and techniques that predate the computer and, in fact, fail to make full use of its information-juggling potential (e.g., Pfaffenberger, forthcoming-b). The concern here is, in sum, with the old and enduring genres of software technology (as well as a few new ones), and I expect them to remain in place for years to come.

2. TECHNOLOGY IN QUALITATIVE RESEARCH: AN OVERVIEW

Despite a major shift toward quantitative analyses in the decades following World War II (Collins, 1975), no obituary has yet appeared for *qualitative research,* a research strategy that "fundamentally depends on watching people in their own territory and interacting with them in their own language, on their own terms" (Kirk and Miller, 1986: 1). On the contrary, something of a renaissance is well underway in qualitative research. This renaissance stems, or so argues the anthropologist

Clifford Geertz, from scholars' interest in looking less for the "sort of thing that connects planets and pendulums" and more "for the sort that connects chrysanthemums and swords" (Winkler, 1985: 5). Qualitative studies, at their best, provide the inside view of social behavior—the meaningful "connecting links" (Smith and Manning, 1982: xviii)—that make the observable (and quantifiable) patterns of behavior intelligible to the observer.

Social scientists who use qualitative strategies, however, face what Sproull and Sproull (1982: 283) accurately call a "cruel trade-off" between the richness of qualitative data and the tedium involved in analyzing it (e.g., Miles, 1979: 593-595). Visual anthropology aside, nearly all qualitative techniques produce text, and in copious amounts. To "capture" qualitative data is to write it down, to make it into field notes, life histories, interview transcriptions, case histories, protocol analyses, and rank listings. Acknowledging this point, Geertz (quoted in Lyman, 1984: 75) recently argued that the participant-observer is more accurately described as a participant-writer. Unfortunately, to analyze this textually captured data is to engage in a paper-pushing enterprise of monstrous proportions. If the job is to be done properly, the researcher is in for such tormenting jobs as manually searching thousands of pages of notes for an obscure passage, recoding all the field notes to suit a newly discovered framework of coding categories, and rewriting the notes to flesh out events from memory.

The inherent difficulty of qualitative data analysis keeps qualitative researchers at arm's length from their data and, arguably, it retards the growth of analytical sophistication. Not a few qualitative researchers have brought back reams of data from the field only to ignore the bulk of it. And despite Merton's (1968: 444) call for a new level of discussion and sophistication in qualitative research methods, by 1984 qualitative data analysis still involved little more than "underlining, shuffling paper, rereading, and cutting and pasting" (Conrad and Reinharz, 1984: 7). The very richness of qualitative research is, in short, its bane.

Quantitative researchers used to suffer in much the same way. Before computer statistical packages were devised in the early 1960s, quantitative studies in sociology were all but restricted to small data sets and simple analytical strategies. In 1946, for example, two-thirds of sociology journal articles that employed statistical methods used only totals, percentages, and simple cross-tabulations. Although more sophisticated techniques such as multiple regression analysis were known, they could not be applied without "mechanical calculators and small armies of graduate students to operate them" (Collins, 1982: 439). General-purpose statistical packages such as SPSS, however, put the use of sophisticated techniques (and large data sets) within the reach of any social scientist who had access to a mainframe computer. Overall, the result was an impressive expansion in the quality of survey analysis—even though, as Martin Levin (1986) notes, some researchers have come to rely more on the statistical package's "mindless" ability to cross-tabulate all variables than spend time developing a well-crafted, thoughtful analysis.

Now that high quality text-processing programs are becoming available for qualitative data analysis, it seems likely that qualitative researchers will enjoy the same two benefits that quantitative researchers receive from the computer: the ability, first, to work quickly and conveniently with much larger units of data, and second, to apply more sophisticated analytical techniques. Yet the computer's potential in qualitative research is still just that, a potential. Although qualitative researchers are taking to microcomputers and word processing in huge numbers, the more sophisticated text-processing applications (such as the production of key-word-in-context concordances and word frequency analysis) are seldom used and, in the main, poorly understood. Furthermore, the methodological texts available on such applications (e.g., Hockey, 1980; Oakman, 1984; Feldman and Norman, 1987) concentrate on literary applications to the virtual exclusion of social science topics. A clear need exists for a brief survey of text-processing applications in a social science context. To survey these applications and indicate their advantages for qualitative research is the first goal of this book.

The Need for a Critical Perspective

To realize the promise of text-processing applications for qualitative research fully, however, it is necessary to adopt a critical perspective on this new technology. At the minimum, qualitative researchers should take great care to grasp just what today's hardware and software can be expected to do—and what such tools *cannot* do. Consider, for example, the fact that computers represent and process text as if it were data in the most general sense—that is, an inherently *meaningless* collection of representations. The word CAT for instance, is represented, stored, and processed as a sequence (a "string," in computer parlance) of three binary numbers. What is not stored is all the information that allows us to make the connection between those three letters and such things as crunchies, Garfield, kitty litter, and a Broadway show. Efforts to represent such connections have made impressive strides in recent years, but the formidable complexity of human semantic systems ensures that a meaning-sensitive text-processing technology is still many years away—if, indeed, it is feasible at all. In practice, therefore, a qualitative researcher must understand that a computer-assisted search of a text for the word BIRTH will retrieve all passages in which the string BIRTH appears; however, it will not retrieve passages that mention PARTURI-TION but omit BIRTH—unless it is specifically instructed to do so. So long as limitations of this sort are clearly understood, search techniques and other applications can be used with some profit. The second goal of this book, therefore, is to assess the limitations of the text-processing applications available for qualitative research.

There is more to a critical perspective on technology, however, than a mere awareness of an application's limitations. Such an approach requires reflection about the computer's likely impact on qualitative research. After all, quantitative social scientists still wonder whether the computer, rather than people, has dictated the trajectory of sociological theory in recent decades (Levin, 1986). To approach this question, however, requires nothing less than a complete rethinking of the culturally provided views we tend to hold on the relationship between technology and social behavior.

Studies of Western views of this relationship reveal two propositions that, on the surface, appear to be grossly contradictory. The first, which Winner (1986: 5-6) calls *technological somnambulism,* holds that the human relationship to technology is simply "too obvious to merit serious reflection." It consists only of "making," which is of interest only to engineers and technicians, and "use," which amounts only to an "occasional, innocuous, [and] nonstructuring occurrence." Use is understood to be a straightforward matter: You pick up a tool, use it, and put it down. In this view, a given technology is by definition culturally, morally, and politically neutral. It is, as Buchanan (1965: 163) puts it, "essentially amoral, an instrument which can be used for good or ill," and so the impact of a technology depends on the ethical awareness of the people using it.

The second proposition, *technological determinism,* takes what appears to be precisely the opposite position, namely, that technology is a powerful and autonomous agent that dictates in some detail the patterns of human social and cultural life (e.g., White, 1959)—and usually for the worse. Modern technology, moreover, is often assumed to be even more autonomous—indeed, out of control—since it unfolds along a pathway afforded by the "grand avenue" of scientific advance (Ellul, 1962). Civilization, in this view, is yoked to a runaway beast that is stripping us of our humanity: the cold, detached values of scientific technology (efficiency and economy) have taken precedence over aesthetic values, respect for the environment, and concern for social justice. Folk versions of this view take the form of assertions such as "the use of computers is depersonalizing and isolating."

Underlying the apparent contradiction, however, is—surprisingly—a hidden unity: Both views gravely understate or disguise the *social* dimension of technology (Pfaffenberger, forthcoming-a). Both see technology as an autonomous thing; it either has no relationship to society (technological somnambulism) or stands to society as does an independent variable to a dependent variable (technological determinism). This view represents a remarkable denial of the human dimension of technology; to put it in Marxist terms, technology is *fetishized.* What is in reality produced by relations among people appears before us in a fantastic form as relations among things (Godelier, 1972: xxv).

Yet this human dimension is becoming increasingly readable as scholars strip away the facade of ideology that disguises it. Increasingly, technology is defined, not as material culture (e.g., a thing), but as a socially and culturally constituted system of knowledge (Layton, 1974) and social relationships. And its "impact on society" is coming to be studied, not on the basis of the simplistic assumptions of technological somnambulism or determinism, but by terms supplied by the sociology of scientific knowledge (Pinch and Bijker, 1984). The sociology of science demonstrates that scientific "truth" is socially constructed by political processes of academic negotiation (Mulkay, 1979) and, what is more, by the surrounding culture's prominent role in providing metaphors and analogies for the expression or constitution of scientific "facts" (e.g., Holton, 1973; Manning, 1979). Radical interpretations of this evidence go so far as to deny that science possesses a privileged epistemological status; it is simply one "knowledge culture" among others (Collins and Pinch, 1979). Such perspectives amount to a refusal to accept science's myths about itself at face value (Goonatilake, 1984).

Technology is socially constructed in precisely the same way, and it therefore deserves the same kind of analysis. The myth that technology advances uncontrollably along a "grand avenue" made possible by scientific advances has been shown to be misleading, if not false, in numerous studies. Noble (1986), for instance, has shown that, as new technologies are developed, engineers confront a variety of design options. Pressures external to the design process itself—economic considerations, management goals, and even culturally defined notions of how a technology should be used—impinge on the selection of one option over another. In his important book, Noble shows how American companies rejected a GE-developed machine tool automation system called record/playback in favor of numerical control systems. The record/playback system required the service of a highly skilled machinist, whose movements would be recorded and, later, played back automatically. Corporate management, however, was more interested in an approach to industrial automation that could eliminate skilled (and unionized) machinists altogether, replacing them by nonunionized, semiskilled "button pushers." Numerical control techniques did precisely that, and more: they took decision-making power away from workers and put it in the hands of central management. For engineers, too, such techniques had the additional appeal of "technical sweetness"; computerized numerical control techniques were clearly the wave of the future, while record/playback was merely an attempt to capture the past. Industrial automation, in sum, could have preserved a role for well-paid, skilled machinists; that it did not do so testifies to the role of social choices in shaping the technology we end up getting.

Once created, however, the opportunity for social choice diminishes. An implemented technology carries with it a powerful vision of the society in which it is to be used, replete with an equally powerful endowment of symbolic meaning and, sometimes, an obligatory plan for the way people will have to arrange themselves to use it. A technology thus embodies what Noble (1986: xi) calls a "frozen fragment of human and social endeavor," replete with a set of values, a vision of how the technology should be used, and often a plan for the social relationships required to weave the technology into human life. It presents us with what Winner (1986) calls a "form of life," a set of social and symbolic circumstances in which people—to the extent that they adopt the technology—are more or less obliged to carry on their daily affairs.

To make this point, however, is not to assume—as would a technological determinist—that the impact of a given technology is certain or that it will everywhere be the same. Such an argument would be specious, for reasons that deserve clarification here. Technological determinism holds, in essence, that the independent variable, technology (i.e., a thing, something extraneous to society) affects the dependent variable, society. Yet—textbook definitions of technology aside—the new studies in the history of technology have shown that technology is not a thing, an object external to social behavior. On the contrary, technology *is* social behavior. If technology is social behavior, then in assessing its impact we are not talking about the impact of a "thing" on "society." We are talking about the *relationship between one form of social behavior and others* (MacKenzie and Wajcman, 1985: 3). This relationship is complex, shot through with meaning, indeterminate, and—one might add—a perfect subject in itself for interpretive, qualitative analysis.

These new findings in the history and sociology of technology are of more than passing relevance to the use of computer hardware and software in qualitative research. The hallmark of qualitative studies, after all, is their careful concern with epistemological issues; to do qualitative research well means becoming aware of what Bob Scholte calls "pre-understandings," the tacit social assumptions, cultural biases, and outright prejudices that we carry to the field (Scholte, 1974: 441). What these new findings have made clear is that technology is loaded with preunderstandings—and what is more, they are all the more dangerous because they are denied, hidden, and submerged from view in ordinary, day-to-day discourse. To use a microcomputer in qualitative research, then, is to use a form of social behavior whose most remarkable characteristic is its built-in denial that it is a form of social behavior, coupled with its simultaneous symbolic assertion that it is, instead, a disembodied thing. What we must consider, then, as Godelier (1972: xxv) puts it perfectly, is

> the effect *in* and for consciousness of the disguising of social relations *in* and *behind* their appearances. Now these appearances are the *necessary* point of departure of the representations of their . . . relations that individuals *spontaneously* form for themselves. Such images thus constitute the social reality within which these individuals live, and serve them as a means of *acting* within and upon this social reality.

In short, when we introduce a microcomputer into the heart of qualitative research, namely, writing and rewriting, we are acting in a social and symbolic system that is founded on the denial of the technology's social and symbolic aspects. The responsible use of this technology requires, therefore, considerable efforts in the direction of what Scholte (1974) calls "hermeneutical reflection and concern for epistemological error." Such efforts are the hallmark of qualitative studies anyway, but there is ample reason—as the foregoing argument should make clear—to turn an especially wary eye on microcomputer hardware and software.

An example should help to demonstrate that the foregoing is more than academic hot air and that there really is a need for this critical approach to microcomputing. The sine qua non of scholarly involvement in computing is, of course, word processing. In the grip of somnambulism, writers typically regard word processing programs as straightforward and handy tools for the creation, revision, and printing of text. Alternatively, they view the technology as a new, even revolutionary, device that will all but automatically raise their productivity or improve their writing (the determinist view). What they do *not* tend to perceive, however, is word processing's curious (and depressing) social history, and what is more, the compelling evidence that this social history has endowed word processing programs with characteristics that are empirically verifiable to be inimical to the writing process.

Word processing software was initially developed with the engineering ethos in mind—namely, to rescue people from mindless drudgery, and so to benefit civilization. This laudable goal, one that engineers profess with evident conviction, takes on a more sinister implication in the hands of some managers, who sometimes see labor-saving or "user friendly" technologies as opportunities to "deskill" workers. It takes a skilled typist to produce a handsomely formatted typescript with letter perfect formatting; the word processor, however, handles all the difficult formatting operations automatically and relieves the operator of the need for spelling skills. All that is required of the word processor operator is speed—and to make sure the speed is achieved consistently, office word processors are increasingly networked or monitored so that a supervisor can accurately determine a typist's performance. As one such supervisor commented proudly to Jane Barker and Hazel Downing (1985: 160), this technology and its supervisorial regime produces results so that "a less experienced typist is able to produce the same quality of work as a really skilled girl (sic) and almost as quickly."

Word processing was designed, in short, to collapse the time float between the *typing* of a manuscript and the production of a well-formatted, attractive-looking printout. This goal was accomplished, in part, by removing the human dimension of skill as an intervening variable between keyboarding and printing. And it does its job quite well. The more recent achievements in this area include "what-you-see-is-what-you-get" word processing software and desktop publishing software, which graphically (and accurately) represents the printed page on the screen. What is far from clear, however, is whether this technology—which was shaped by the social and economic environment in which it arose—is an effective tool for *writing*.

When word processing software became widely available for microcomputers, there was no end to the gushing enthusiasm with which people involved in writing—writers and writing teachers—received the technology. By making text revision vastly easier and facilitating the production of multiple drafts, word processing would encourage writers to produce higher quality work. Carefully controlled experiments on the use of word processing software in composition instruction have, however, produced disappointing results (e.g., Collier, 1983). One study even found that students do more revision when they use pencils and paper! The reasons for these results are just now becoming clear (Pfaffenberger, 1987). Word processing software was designed for typists, not writers; a typist need see only the section of a page being typed, but a writer (as research on the composing process has revealed) needs to cycle back and forth between writing the text and reviewing the document's structure (Flower and Hayes, 1981). Archaic though they may be, pieces of paper are vastly superior to the limited view of a text that one gets on a 24-line computer display; it is far easier to see the overall structure of a piece when one can flip easily among loose pages. Of course, a writer using word processing software can easily print the document for review, but here another problem emerges: the automatic text formatting capabilities of the software produce what appears to be a beautifully printed, finished document, tacitly introducing the authority of the printed text into the writing process at a premature stage. Word processing, in sum, defeats the writing process by focusing the writer's attention on words and sentences and, when revision is contemplated, by presenting the writer with a typescript that powerfully symbolizes completed work.

The key point here is that once a writer becomes conscious of these built-in, socially shaped characteristics of word processing, it is quite easy to devise strategies to mitigate their ill consequences. Once you know, for instance, that word processing programs tend to concentrate revision efforts on the word and sentence levels to the detriment of overall structural coherence, it is obvious that you should pay more attention to the structure of large text domains when using a word processing program. The authoritative appearance of the well-formatted document can be similarly combated by such strategies as printing on yellow paper (suggesting that the text is a draft) or eschewing right margin justification and other symbols of finished work.

The cure for all such problems, in sum, is critical awareness—relentless critical awareness. A technology is like a colonial power—it tells you that it is working in your best interests and, all the while, it is functioning insidiously to dim your critical perception of the world around you. You will remain its victim so long as you fail to conceptualize adequately what it's up to. The third goal of this book, then, is to point out these built-in, socially shaped liabilities of text-processing software, and to suggest ways to negate the tacit effect that they may otherwise have on a qualitative researcher's work.

It should be stressed that no attempt is made here to introduce the reader to microcomputers or academic word processing (see, instead, Pfaffenberger, 1986 or, for a treatment designed for literary scholars, Feldman and Norman, 1987); nor will "how-to" instruction be found for specific software packages. Moreover, some familiarity with micro-computers and, at the minimum, word processing is assumed. Finally, this book is not intended to discuss or evaluate specific microcomputers or microcomputer programs. Where software is discussed, the approach taken is generic and conceptual: for instance, the chapters to follow survey and evaluate such software options as automatic indexers, text-oriented data base managers, and key-word-in-context (KWIC) concordance generation programs. Where specific programs such as ZyIndex, Notebook II, and WordCruncher are mentioned, the intention is merely to illustrate the properties (and preunderstandings) that are common to all or most programs of their type. Specific programs will, after all, come and go, but the generic categories into which such programs can be placed show a stability that counters the intuitive assumption of volatility and innovation in the microcomputer market-place. This pattern is now quite clear in the business market, where the features and performance of relational data base managers, multifunc-tion spreadsheet packages, and professional word processing programs have stabilized to a remarkable degree and can be discussed profitably in generic terms, even for training purposes (for an example of such an approach, see Pfaffenberger, 1987a).

Why Microcomputers?

Although larger computers have been (and will continue to be) useful for qualitative research applications, microcomputers have three major advantages for qualitative research.

First, battery-powered (but still quite powerful) microcomputers can be taken directly to the field, where they can be used for the *direct entry* of field notes, interview transcriptions, and the like. The significance of this point cannot be overstated. The major obstacle to computer-assisted applications in qualitative research prior to the microcomputer was the expense of transcribing huge quantities of handwritten or typed field notes to computer-readable form. To be sure, optical character reading (OCR) devices such as the Kurzweil 4000 can automatically create transcriptions from clean typescript, but the better OCR machines are expensive, the transcription process is slow and tedious, and even the best ones will make errors. It makes much more sense to write up the notes in computer-readable form in the first place.

Some fieldworkers will prefer not to bring portable computers into field research situations, fearing that the machine would intrude on the observation process (e.g., Lyman, 1984). Even so, there are still good grounds to recommend the use of portable computers and the direct entry of field notes, insofar as it is possible: The notes taken during field observation sessions are usually cryptic, so retyping them into the computer immediately afterwards will not add significantly to the paperwork dimension of fieldwork. The more copious field notes, such as after-the-fact reflections and field journals, are usually created after the field session is over for the day. These notes can be entered directly into the computer without qualms.

One other potential problem with computer-based research notes deserves mention here. To use a microcomputer to store field notes is to transform the experience of a social world into lexical form—or more specifically, into lexical forms that can be keyboarded (Altheide, 1985). As such, it biases a researcher's note-taking activities against some fruitful nontextual exercises, such as those described by an anthropologist: "I'm always drawing diagrams, sketching things, describing the theater of things. . . . If you are writing longhand, rich designs can flow directly from the material you are working with" (quoted in Lyman, 1984: 83). Typing one's notes into the computer, at least with most programs, strips away the graphics. The cure is to realize that there may still be a place for handwriting, doodling, and graphically "describing the theater of things" even in a highly computerized research operation. There's no reason to restrict one's note-taking activities to the computer when drawing sketches on paper may still have a place in the research.

The second advantage of microcomputers for qualitative researchers is that a surprisingly wide variety of useful (and inexpensive) application packages are available in microcomputer formats. Software originally intended for business purposes, such as word processing and data base management programs, are useful for qualitative computing (so long as their limitations are kept in mind). And software developed specifically for literary analysis and qualitative computing, such as key-word-in-context concordance programs, is now making its migration from mainframe to microcomputer formats. And all the while, microcomputers are becoming smaller, cheaper, more portable, and more powerful.

The third advantage of microcomputers is that, owing to their low cost, social scientists can afford to own them outright. Collins (1982) underscores the significance of this point in Marxist terms: To own a microcomputer is, for a computer-using social scientist, to own and control the scholarly means of production. To use a mainframe, in contrast, means paying stiff timesharing costs ("renting the means of production") that discourage exploratory data analysis. It may also mean accepting the software-purchasing decisions of an academic computing center, which is all but certain to have priorities that differ from the researcher's. And as Peter Lyman (1984) found to his dismay, using a mainframe may even mean accepting the possibility that a technically adept intruder—that is, a "hacker"—could gain access to one's field notes, thus violating their confidentiality. To own one's own microcomputer is, in a way that is far from trivial, to control one's own means of knowledge production.

Microcomputers, in sum, are ideally suited for qualitative research, but it bears mentioning that—like any research technology—it makes good sense to scrutinize the preunderstandings that they bring to the research process. And here we are much informed by the work of Sherry Turkle (1980, 1982). In interviewing dozens of personal computer users, Turkle encountered some men who seem to have become trapped by the machine: They saw in it a comforting but infantile world of retreat, in which it was possible to establish the total control, coupled with a sense of prowess and achievement, that could not be achieved in social life. Turkle notes that, although these men felt that becoming adept at the computer gave them an enhanced sense of self-esteem and competence, it was a Pyrrhic victory: The world they had conquered—a world of amateur programming and adventure games—bore little relation to the world of social relations and did nothing to improve their competence there.

Turkle's work clearly sounds a warning note: The microcomputer is known to have snared some men in something of a psychological trap. Yet there are grounds, I would argue, to sound a more general alarm. The men Turkle interviewed clearly saw the microcomputer as an instrument by which they could create their own rite of passage, moving themselves to a new status in which they saw themselves as more competent, more efficacious, and more in control. In this context, one can only note Cynthia Cockburn's argument (1985) that for men in Western culture, this is precisely the role provided by all forms of highly sophisticated technical expertise: It is, she argues, a key element of men's "formative processes" and becomes, once acquired, men's "social property." To use the microcomputer, then, is to use a symbol that tacitly communicates meanings of potency, male prowess, control, legitimacy, efficacy, expertise, and achievement. As Michael Agar puts it (1983), to use the microcomputer is tantamount to speaking in what Bernstein would call an elaborated code, a code that is so closely associated with intelligence and competence that it impresses people, even if you use it to state the obvious.

It should now be clear why so much work involving the computer in social science amounts, as critics often say, to the study of trivial issues with highly sophisticated techniques. In the academic environment, where survival requires constructing an impression of competence, using the computer is as irresistible as using other socially meaningful symbols of scientific or scholarly competence, such as big words and the passive voice. Trouble starts, however, when the concern for elaborating the code overwhelms concern for the substance of what is being said.

There's no easy formula for knowing when you've lost the necessary perspective, although the expenditure of large amounts of unproductive time in front of a computer display screen is suggestive. The point of applying the computer to qualitative research, after all, is not to become involved in the microcomputer, but on the contrary to become involved in the research data. So long as the microcomputer furthers and deepens that involvement, it is playing a positive role. But when the microcomputer starts to loom larger in significance than the original goals of the research, when it demands less engagement in the research data and more engagement in the computer, the time has come to reflect on these goals and to reestablish contact with the values and commitments that initially motivated your engagement with the human social world.

3. FIELD NOTES:
STRATEGIES FOR THE STORAGE
AND RETRIEVAL OF TEXTUAL DATA

A major advantage of the computer, as was foreseen by Ada Augusta (1815-1846), a friend of Charles Babbage, the daughter of the poet Byron, and arguably the world's first female computer scientist, is that it can assist us "in making *available* what we are already acquainted with" (cited in Bernstein, 1981: 57). At the minimum, a computer-based system for the storage and retrieval of field notes should permit a researcher to identify, in seconds, all the passages in the corpus of field notes that contain a particular concept.

Yet there is far more to qualitative data analysis than the mere retrieval of data, however fast and accurately it is accomplished. Any microcomputer system used for qualitative research should be able to perform storage and retrieval functions in a way that specifically aids qualitative analysis methods, such as analytic induction (Manning, 1982) and constant comparison (Glaser and Strauss, 1967). This chapter is concerned, then, with the ways that microcomputer application packages can assist the distinctive tasks of qualitative data analysis by improving access to data stored in field notes. Here it is assumed that the analysis itself will take place under human control and direction. The next chapter discusses software approaches that perform (or attempt to perform) some aspects of data analysis automatically.

Field notes are here conceived in the broadest sense as a multifarious body of texts derived from a variety of sources. Qualitative researchers are, after all, likely to bring back a wide variety of materials from the field, including the following (Agar, 1986; Goldschmidt, 1972; Spradley, 1979):

— verbatim transcriptions of observed activity;
— rewritten versions of such transcriptions that are "fleshed out" from memory;
— transcriptions of elicitation sessions, interviews or conversations;
— a fieldwork journal that contains analytical memos, a running record of

analysis and interpretation, and observations on experiences, fears, problems, confusions, breakthroughs, and mistakes that occur as the fieldwork progresses; and
— notes on written sources, such as popular novels, published autobiographies, or archival materials.

Whatever their origin, these materials are of value only when they are readily available for retrospective write-up once the research is complete. The field notes themselves, after all, are of value only as a chronicle of an emerging grasp of a cultural setting, a grasp that fosters a mode of interpretation in which everything in the recorded "facts" appears in a new light. It's precisely when such an interpretation emerges that the recorded materials realize their true value, namely, as potent stimuli to one's memory and as a fund of case examples. This interpretation guides the write-up, which is enriched (and comes to life) only to the extent that *all* potentially relevant materials are retrieved quickly, accurately, and when they are needed.

The best qualitative data analyses take full advantage of the richness and diversity of the materials deriving from the field encounter. They consider all potentially relevant materials at the same time, whether they derive from naturalistic observations or notes taken on a particularly useful work of fiction. The aim of this chapter, therefore, is to survey and evaluate microcomputer approaches to the storage and retrieval of field notes that treat the entire mass of such materials as a single corpus.

A corpus of field notes comprising such a wide variety of materials is bound to be voluminous. Indeed, many researchers return from the field with thousands of pages of such notes. Until recently, it would have been absurd to suggest that a microcomputer system, let alone a portable one, would have sufficient data storage and processing capabilities to handle such a massive amount of material. Yet the hardware problem has been solved. The proliferation and ready availability of fast microprocessor chips, coupled with a dramatic fall in the cost of internal memory chips and hard disks, have laid the technical foundation for a comprehensive microcomputer approach to field notes. Most qualitative researchers will find that it is the software, not the hardware, that calls on them to make hard choices. This chapter is intended, in part, to clarify the costs and benefits of the various software options. In order to do so, it is necessary to begin by reflecting on the nature and strategies of qualitative data analysis. Just what is it that qualitative researchers do when they sit down to analyze a huge mass of field notes?

The Nature of Qualitative Analysis

As many social researchers have observed, the techniques of qualitative data analysis rank among the least explicitly formulated of all research methods (Miles, 1979). Indeed, some who attempt to systematize such methods remark in despair, as did Blaxter (1979: 650), that the definition of qualitative data analysis techniques is that they are "innovative, exploratory, and individual." Even so, it is clear that qualitative data analysis, like any other form of analysis, requires that the material be broken down into its constituent elements, which must be compared, named, and classified so that their nature and interaction becomes clear. In qualitative studies, this process usually involves three activities: *rewriting, coding,* and *comparison.* The computer system chosen for qualitative research purposes should encourage and foster these analytic activities. As will be seen, they are the backbone of discovery and theoretical sophistication in qualitative studies.

Rewriting. Field researchers frequently rewrite their notes, filling in their initial impressions from memory with more detail—and for good reason. Since there is seldom enough time in a field session to take detailed notes, most researchers like to "flesh out" the day's field notes by reworking and expanding them immediately after the session (Spradley, 1979). The retrospective rewriting of field notes, however, does far more than serve as a mere pretext for stimulating one's memory. Such acts of rewriting are an important form of data analysis and theoretical discovery in themselves. The rewriting of one's field notes provides an opportunity, for instance, to fill in the culturally provided, contextual knowledge that may be missing from the actual statements that informants make in field research encounters.

Such knowledge is often left unstated when people talk. Halliday and Hasan (1976), in fact, argue that the coherence of a text—any unit of spoken or written language—ultimately depends only partly on its internal coherence (which is a rhetorical matter). Of decisive importance, too, are tacit references to what they call exophora, or references to culturally defined world knowledge. The statements made by informants and recorded in a researcher's field notes, then, are—at least from the researcher's viewpoint—incomplete; they cannot become coherent for the researcher (and the researcher's audience) until all the tacit references to cultural knowledge are made explicit and explained.

When Colin Turnbull (1962) worked among the BaMbuti Pygmies, for instance, a skeptical hunter asked his companion the following question after Turnbull returned from a forest outing: "Did he keep up with the others, or did he walk like the BaNgwana?" (p. 79). The reference to the BaNgwana is exophoric. It omits something that is presumed (e.g., cultural knowledge of how the BaNgwana walk, and what that means to the studied population), but it tacitly refers to it.

Such references may be utterly unclear to the field researcher—and this is fruitful, to the extent that the researcher must seek further knowledge to clarify them. They tend to produce what Agar (1986: 20) calls a breakdown, a perception by the fieldworker that something does not make sense—that it is, at least from the fieldworker's cultural perspective, incoherent. A breakdown, in essence, is a "lack of fit between one's encounter with a tradition and the schema-guided expectations by which one organizes experience" (p. 21). The field ethnographer tries to resolve breakdowns by creating a new schema, one that integrates or resolves the puzzling or insensible behavior. The discovery of the new schema brings with it additional world knowledge, which can be fed back into the field notes to explain puzzling statements or seemingly inexplicable behavior.

The rewriting of field notes, in short, is an integral part of field research itself. This fact argues for a computerized field note storage and retrieval system that does not punish the researcher who alters field notes repeatedly. As will be seen, some software approaches punish the fieldworker in precisely this way by making efficient retrieval operations dependent on time-consuming, cumbersome reindexing procedures every time the field notes are altered.

Coding. Coding is the process of attaching category names to the basic units of field research data (Glaser, 1978; Charmaz, 1983), the units that Agar (1986) calls a *strip*. That such units exist, and that their integrity is of fundamental importance, deserves some elaboration here.

A strip, in Agar's definition, is any field research experience that is, in essence, a "bounded phenomenon." The boundaries can be supplied by the host culture or by the field researcher. When supplied by the host culture, a unit of social behavior is a strip to the extent, claims Agar, that it is "recognizable as a unit by the nature of its characterization in the informant's language" (27). Field researchers mark the boundaries of strips themselves, too, when they conduct informal or formal interviews or observations or take notes on a work of literature or a document in a historical archive. Such strips still have a phenomenological unity, even if it is imposed by external factors rather than arising sui generis from the flow of social behavior.

TABLE 1
Some Coding Strategies

Prefer inclusive codes to exclusive ones. The point of coding is to interlink units of data. The interlinkages thus created will play a major role in data analysis. To maximize the number of such interlinkages, use inclusive codes—codes that link at least two (and preferably many) strips together. The point is, that in any subsequent sifting of data, such codes will be more likely to include a relevant item than to leave it out. Try to code each strip, moreover, with two or more codes.

Let coding categories emerge from the data. Mark off coherent stretches of the field notes by the topical focus expressed in them. Question the a priori, exogenous categories developed before field research (such as "pilgrimage" and "ritual"). If such categories obscure indigenous ones, and if the indigenous ones fit the data better, replace the exogenous categories with those recognized and used by the studied culture or organization.

Develop abstract categories. The exclusive use of indigenous categories makes it difficult to compare your data with cases derived from other contexts. While developing indigenous categories, therefore, strive also to find abstract categories (e.g., "legitimation" or "rite of passage") that *do* fit the data, and apply them to all relevant instances.

Classify data and create typologies. Using both indigenous and exogenous categories, subdivide and classify the data. Develop a framework that links the codes together typologically.

Change and refine the categories as understanding improves. The achievement of a workable framework of codes, one that is sensitive to patterns in the data and does the best possible job of linking related data, is itself a form of theoretical discovery.

SOURCES: Agar (1983), Becker and Geer (1960), Becker, Gordon, and LeBailly (1984), Glaser and Strauss (1967), Podolefsky and McCarty (1983).

The coding categories given to strips may initially stem from exogenous analytical frameworks (e.g., *pilgrimage* or *devotional ceremony*), but they will almost certainly be modified—often by the substitution of indigenous categories—as the research progresses. In fact, this process of modification, in which these concepts are honed and subdivided to suit the new understanding of the data that is emerging, is in itself an essential part of qualitative data analysis. As the researcher discovers new codes and creates typologies to sort the data (Table 1), a framework of theory—*grounded theory,* in Glaser and Strauss's (1967) terms—emerges from the field research encounter. To counter the potential for theoretical solipsism inherent in using progressively more indigenous categories, however, most methodology handbooks recommend the reintroduction of more general, nonindigenous analytic terms (e.g., *legitimation* or *marital alliance*), so long as the researcher is sure

TABLE 2
Some Heuristic Strategies for Qualitative Data Analysis

Refining codes. While coding an incident of social behavior with a category, think about previous instances of the incident that are coded the same way (and look at some of them). Is the code really appropriate for all these instances?

Determining the essential features of a phenomenon. Look at all of the strips to which a particular subject code (such as "pilgrimage" or "violence") has been attached. What other behaviors or situations are always present when the coded behavior is present? If so, are the associated behaviors or situations the *cause* of the behavior? Are they the *consequences* of the behavior?

Generalizations. To test the validity of a generalization about a form of social behavior, look at all the strips that contain the behavior's code. Does the generalization hold true for all cases? Are there any negative cases in which the putative causal agent is missing? If a negative case is found, how should the generalization be modified?

Extreme-bias cases. Are there any strips that show evidence of self-interested parties agreeing with your interpretation, even though it cuts across the grain of their interests or biases? If so, your interpretation gains added weight.

Prediction. Given your generalization, try to predict what else would be true if your generalization were true.

SOURCES: Miles (1979), Manning (1982).

that the use of these terms will not vitiate a more culturally sensitive understanding of the data. At the minimum, then, a microcomputer system for the storage, retrieval, and analysis of field notes should permit the researcher to use a *flexible* and *evolving* set of coding categories (Brent, 1984: 35-36). And as will be seen, a second and related requirement is that the retrieval technique should respect the integrity of the strip as a coherent unit.

Comparison. The emergence of grounded theory from the data does not stem from the mere act of fixing codes to strips; it requires *comparing* similarly coded strips (Table 2). Comparison generates theory. In the analytic strategy called *analytic induction* (Manning, 1982), for instance, all similarly coded instances of a category are examined together to determine which features of social behavior are always present when the coded phenomenon is present. In the *constant comparison method* advocated by Glaser and Strauss (1967), the comparison is not put off until the "research" is finished and the "analysis" begins. All new notes are written only after looking back at previously written notes bearing the same code (Glaser, 1967: 107-109). Both analytical methods require, in short, a system that can quickly and easily group similarly coded notes together into a unit. In case the codes change, however, such groupings should be temporary and subject to easy alteration.

With these requirements for qualitative analysis in mind, this chapter will now survey the options for the storage, retrieval, and analysis of field notes. Qualitative researchers can choose between three basic software strategies for the creation, storage, and retrieval of field notes: (1) using a word processing program to create text files; (2) using an automatic indexing storage and retrieval program to improve the retrieval of notes from the text files; and (3) using a text-oriented data base management program. As will be seen, word processing packages come close to the ideal for creating and storing field notes, but they limit retrieval and analysis. Next examined are automatic indexing programs, which can enhance data retrieval from word processor text files if their potential liabilities are well understood and deliberate steps are taken to overcome them. Finally, text-oriented data base management programs will be seen to offer several advantages for qualitative research.

Word Processing Software and Field Notes

Most qualitative researchers use word processing programs for creating and storing field notes, and for obvious reasons: Such programs offer numerous advantages, not the least of which is their familiarity. Using such software for qualitative research minimizes the learning curve and the risk of data losses due to command errors. Moreover, word processing programs are designed to aid the creation and revision of text. They are ideally suited, therefore, to the first of the three analytic tasks already discussed, the retrospective rewriting of field notes. The problems come later, when the researcher tries to retrieve and analyze the notes.

Figure 1 illustrates another advantage of using a word processing program for recording field notes: flexibility. The program imposes no fixed structure on the record, permitting the researcher to devise a structure that best suits the occasion. In these notes, standard diacritical conventions for field notes (Figure 2) are used for a verbatim account, that is, an account of what happened in a day's observation of social behavior. (Both examples are drawn from my work on pilgrimage, ritual, casts, and ethnic relations in Sri Lanka, see Pfaffenberger, 1979, 1982, 1982, 1983, 1988.)

Using a word processing program's commands for inserting new text within an existing document, a researcher can easily flesh out the day's notes in a retrospective, expanded version. Figure 3 shows an expanded

June 11, 1982
Nainativu, Sri Lanka
Nakapucanai Amman Temple
Verbatim Account No. 27

(Standing out in front of temple, watching ferry boats arrive from the mainland—some Hindus coming even though the festival was cancelled)

(A Sinhalese family is getting out of the boat. They're going to the Buddhist dagoba first, and I'll follow)

(At the dagoba)
"For centuries Sinhalese people have been coming here to <Nagadipa> (note: <Nagadipa>/ <Nainativu> = Sinhalese vs. Tamil???) because this is one of three places Lord Buddha visited in Sri Lanka" (he's a Sinhalese businessman, he says)

(The bhikku comes out)
'I know there is trouble, but the Tamil people here know me. They are fine people and I do not fear to be here.'

Figure 1. Verbatim Field Notes with Diacritical Conventions

version of the notes contained in Figure 1; the additions are shown in boldface type. If desired, the verbatim copy can be left intact; the interpolations can be made in a duplicate.

Once the field notes have been expanded retrospectively, the word processing program provides a highly useful tool—the macro function—for coding the data (Gillespie, 1984). Most professional-level word processing packages include a macro function, which allows the user to store and retrieve a recorded series of keystrokes. Most programs allow the user to store an unlimited number of such recorded series of keystrokes. The keystrokes can contain text (such as boilerplate), program commands, or a combination of the two. The macro is set in motion by entering a special command followed by the code name or number that refers to the macro.

The storage of code names in macros has two major advantages over merely typing them into the text. First, entering code names with a macro ensures that each code will always be entered in precisely the same way, with exactly the same spelling. Such consistency is absolutely essential for the accuracy of retrieval operations using computer

Diacritical Mark	Use
" "	contains a verbatim quote
' '	contains a paraphrase
( )	contextual data or interpretation
< >	contains emic word or phrase
————	denotes passage of time
/	denotes emic contrast

Figure 2. Basic Field Note Conventions

searching techniques. If one strip is recorded with the misspelled code ETHNIC INTRACTION instead of the correct ETHNIC INTERAC-TION, it will not be retrieved by a computer search throughout the document for ETHNIC INTERACTION. Second, the use of macros greatly speeds the entry of such codes, which would otherwise have to be entered by typing the same word over and over again.

Since codes are deliberately applied to units of text to name them and categorize them, they should be distinguished from the terms that may occur here and there in the text itself. To understand why, consider a strip in which the researcher notes, in frustration, "I was hoping to learn something about ethnic interaction today, but after sitting and watching for six hours nothing has happened worth noting. I did find out some interesting things about fulfilling vows, though, and I think this deserves more study." This strip is not *about* ethnic interaction, except in the most peripheral sense; it's about fulfilling vows. So it is of only limited value in a set of retrieved documents that are ostensibly about ethnic interaction. To avoid the retrieval of such records, the researcher can use codes that are tied to special marking characters, characters that would be unlikely to occur naturally in the text, such as

ETHNIC INTERACTION

Searching for **ETHNIC INTERACTION** will retrieve only those records that have been *deliberately* encoded with precisely this string of characters. Figure 4 shows the final version of the retrospective, expanded notes; the codes are shown in boldface.

The use of special symbols such as asterisks with codes has another advantage, as well. As the research goes on, the researcher is sure to find that some codes prove unsuitable and need to be renamed. Often, too, the researcher finds that too many codes have been used; in the relevant

June 11, 1982
Nainativu, Sri Lanka
Nakapucanai Amman Temple
Expanded Retrospective Version of Verbatim Account No. 27.

(Standing out in front of temple, watching ferry boats arrive from the mainland—some Hindus coming even though the festival was cancelled—**the festival was cancelled because the temple trustees decided to undertake some badly-needed repairs to the roof, which is sagging and leaking badly. The trustees put an ad in the paper and on the local radio station announcing the cancellation, but they did so—I am told by a bystander—rather tardily and not everyone seems to know about it. The Hindus coming in don't seem to mind; even though the festival's cancelled, they're still going over and worshipping at the temple. Most are evidently coming to fulfill a vow, and you can do that whether or not the festival's still on.**)

(A Sinhalese family is getting out of the boat. **The father is dressed in Western clothes. None of the Tamil Hindu men are dressed in Western clothes; they're all wearing verttis. The mother is wearing a nice, Indian-style sari. The two little boys are wearing schoolboy shirts and shorts.** They're going to the Buddhist dagoba first, and I'll follow—**hey, Tamils go to the Hindu temple first!!!**)

(At the dagoba, **I briefly interviewed the Sinhalese businessman**)
"For centuries Sinhalese people have been coming here to <Nagadipa> (note: <Nagadipa>/ <Nainativu> = Sinhalese vs. Tamil???) because this is one of three places Lord Buddha visited in Sri Lanka" (he's a Sinhalese businessman, he says—**he didn't come here to fulfill a vow, just to get merit**)

(The bhikku comes out. **The Sinhalese businessman, the bhikku, and I get involved in a discussion of the current ethnic problem. The Sinhalese businessman asks the bhikku whether he is frightened to stay here, where almost everyone is Tamil**)
'I know there is trouble, but the Tamil people here know me. They are fine people and I do not fear to be here.'
(**On the way out, and out of earshot of the two Sinhalese, my Tamil field assistant says**)
"He didn't mention that when there is trouble the Navy comes by here to protect him. That is the nature of this Government. They protect the Buddhist temples here, but no Hindu temple gets protection in the South when there is trouble. For this reason many Hindu temples have been badly vandalized."

Figure 3. Expanded, Retrospective Version of Verbatim Notes

June 11, 1982
Nainativu, Sri Lanka
Nakapucanai Amman Temple
Expanded Retrospective Version of Verbatim Account No. 27
Coded June 12, 1982
Major subject codes: **NAINATIVU**
                              ETHNIC INTERACTION
                              ETHNIC DIFFERENTIATION

(Standing out in front of temple, watching ferry boats arrive from the mainland—some Hindus coming even though the festival was cancelled—the festival was cancelled because the temple trustees decided to undertake some badly-needed repairs to the roof, which is sagging and leaking badly. The trustees put an ad in the paper and on the local radio station announcing the cancellation, but they did so—I am told by a bystander—rather tardily and not everyone seems to know about it. The Hindus coming in don't seem to mind; even though the festival's cancelled, they're still going over and worshipping at the temple. Most are evidently coming to fulfill a vow, and you can do that whether or not the festival's still on.) **VOW-FULFILLMENT**

(A Sinhalese family is getting out of the boat. The father is dressed in Western clothes. None of the Tamil Hindu men are dressed in Western clothes; they're all wearing verttis. The mother is wearing a nice, Indian-style sari. The two little boys are wearing schoolboy shirts and shorts. They're going to the Buddhist dagoba first, and I'll follow—hey, Tamils go to the Hindu temple first!!!) **ETHNIC DIFFERENTIATION**

(At the dagoba, I briefly interviewed the Sinhalese businessman)
"For centuries Sinhalese people have been coming here to <Nagadipa> (note: <Nagadipa>/ <Nainativu> = Sinhalese vs. Tamil???) because this is one of three places Lord Buddha visited in Sri Lanka" (he's a Sinhalese businessman, he says—he didn't come here to fulfill a vow, just to get merit) **ETHNIC DIFFERENTIATION** **VOW-FULFILLMENT**

(The bhikku comes out. The Sinhalese businessman, the bhikku, and I get involved in a discussion of the current ethnic problem. The Sinhalese businessman asks the bhikku whether he is frightened to stay here, where almost everyone is Tamil) **ETHNIC CONFLICT**
'I know there is trouble, but the Tamil people here know me. They are fine people and I do not fear to be here.' **ETHNIC INTERACTION**
(On the way out, and out of earshot of the two Sinhalese, my Tamil field assistant says) "He didn't mention that when there is trouble the Navy comes by here to protect him. That is the nature of this Government. They protect the Buddhist temples here, but no Hindu temple gets protection in the South when there is trouble. For this reason many Hindu temples have been badly vandalized." **CONFLICTING PERSPECTIVES**

Figure 4. Coded Version of Notes

figures, for instance, it could turn out that **ETHNIC CONFLICT** and **ETHNIC INTERACTION** are not sufficiently differentiated and have been used unsystematically. A word processing program's search-and-replace command can be used to rename codes automatically throughout the field note corpus. The risk of using such a command, however, is that it may make changes that were not intended. Suppose, for instance, that the researcher wants to change the code "ethnic conflict" to "ethnic interaction" throughout the field note corpus. The program, however, changes not just the codes, but also the words "ethnic conflict" in an informant's statement, thus vitiating the integrity of the data ("The history of Ceylon since 1948 is ethnic conflict and more ethnic conflict" becomes "The history of Ceylon since 1948 is ethnic interaction and more ethnic interaction"). A search and replace operation using the code surrounded by its asterisks (**ETHNIC CONFLICT**), however, will not produce these unintended results.

The advantages of using a word processing program for creating and storing field notes are apparent from the foregoing examples. What is not so apparent, however, is that such programs place a heavy penalty on the user who attempts to use them for retrieving and analyzing the notes thus created.

Most word processing programs do not provide text-searching tools of sufficient power and flexibility to facilitate the retrieval of text for analytical purposes. To be sure, almost all such programs include a simple search command, one that permits the user to find all instances of a given word in the text, one after the other. Some programs allow case-sensitive searches (e.g., a search could retrieve **ETHNIC INTER-ACTION** but not **ethnic interaction**) and other features, such as truncation (a search for **soc** would retrieve **social, societal, sociable,** and so on). However, such search commands usually do not offer advanced searching features such as the use of Boolean operators (OR, AND, and NOT). Boolean operators enable the researcher to achieve a high degree of control over the breadth of search questions, and they should be considered to be the sine qua non of a field researcher's computer tools.

The OR operator is inclusive; it retrieves all records that meet either criterion specified in a search question. The search question

ETHNIC DIFFERENTIATION **OR** **ETHNIC CONFLICT**

tells the computer, in effect, "Show me all the records that contain the code **ETHNIC DIFFERENTIATION** OR the code **CON-FLICTING PERSPECTIVES**."

The AND operator, in contrast, is exclusive. The search question

ETHNIC DIFFERENTIATION AND **ETHNIC CONFLICT**

will return *only* those records that contain *both* codes.

The NOT operator is also exclusive, but in a different way. The search question

ETHNIC DIFFERENTIATION NOT **NAINATIVU**

returns all the records coded with **ETHNIC DIFFERENTIATION** except the ones that *also* contain the code **NAINATIVU**.

The use of a word processing program for data analysis, in sum, condemns the field researcher to slow, sequential searches for a single term. To be sure, this approach is still superior to a manual search through printed or handwritten notes. But a more serious retrieval problem is encountered when field notes grow voluminous enough to require the use of two or more separate text files—as they surely will. Most microcomputer word processing programs perform sluggishly with text files larger than the equivalent of 50 or 100 double-spaced pages, and some place maximum limits on the length of text files. So most field researchers will find themselves storing their notes in several—perhaps dozens or even hundreds—of separate text files.

In one sense, the multiplicity of files is an advantage: there is no upward limit to the size of the research notes data base one can create with a word processing program, because one can simply keep on creating new text files on new floppy disks. Yet, as many field researchers have discovered, keeping track of these myriad files (and what is in them) can become a vexing task. Currently available microcomputer operating systems (OS) do not do a good job of making huge numbers of text files readily available (or of indicating their contents). An operating system is designed to give the user the tools needed to store and retrieve text and other files on disk. The limitations of microcomputer operating systems are, in part, technical; most had their origins in the days when internal memories were small and memory chips expensive. Yet there is another reason for their poor performance in retrieving text files, a reason that has to do with the social circumstances in which microcomputer word processing first arose.

Microcomputer word processing packages were initially created for two purposes, neither of which required an operating system adept in handling the storage and retrieval of large numbers of text files. The first purpose was to assist computer programmers by providing a way of writing up source code, which would later be compiled into a functioning computer program. Of interest to the programmer is the *current* version of the source code, the exact one that is compiled into the functioning program. All previous versions of the source code are suspect because they contain coding errors. There is, then, only one authoritative text file, the latest and best version of the source code, and its point is to create something else, a compiled version of the program.

The second use of early word processing software was to create technical documentation for computer programs. Many word processing program functions (such as automatic generation of tables of contents and indexes) have their origin in this application. Here, too, there is only one text file that is of interest, the authoritative file that contains the current documentation, and (like source code) it is not in itself the ultimate product: its point is to generate a print-based manual.

In short, microcomputer word processing programs, and the file-handling environments created for them, were not designed to handle dozens or even hundreds of files. On the contrary, they were designed to aid programmers and technical writers who were concerned to keep a limited number of files in an authoritative state. A field researcher who tries to create field notes with a word processing program may well find himself or herself struggling to keep track of dozens or even hundreds of text files, the contents of which may become a mystery. Under such circumstances, the loss of field data—perhaps irretrievably—is not only possible, but probable.

There are ways around this problem, to be sure. One is to create an extensive hand record-keeping system to keep track of disk files (see, e.g., Freidheim, 1984), coupled with sedulous backup procedures (both on floppy disks and hard copy). Such procedures should be followed in any case. The second approach, however, is to use an automatic *indexing* program such as ZyIndex, the purpose of which is to provide precisely the document control procedures that microcomputer operating systems lack.

Automatic Indexers

The shortcomings of microcomputer word processing programs and disk operating systems quickly became evident when the technology migrated out of the programming environment. With the advent of high-capacity hard disks, users began complaining of wading through impenetrable wildernesses of hundreds of cryptically named files. It was in precisely these circumstances that automatic indexing storage and retrieval programs for text files arose.

Such programs have two modes. The first, the indexing mode, creates a single index, called an *inverted file,* to all the words contained on up to several hundred floppy disks. (One such program is capable of indexing 20,000 files, each containing 125,000 characters of text.) The index contains all the unique words used in all the files as well as pointers to the words' locations. The indexing operation is slow; depending on the number and size of the text files to be indexed, it can take as much as several hours to complete.

Once the index has been compiled, however, the information contained in the files can be located quickly using the program's second mode, the retrieval mode. When the user employs this mode to search for a word or words, the program does not search the files themselves (as a word processor's search function does), it searches the index, so retrieval operations are rapid. One such program can search through 10,000 pages of text (in effect) in fewer than five seconds. When the program completes the search, it compiles a list of "hits" and instructs the user to insert the disks containing the correct files. The program then displays the paragraphs within these files that contain the search word or words. If desired, the search can employ Boolean operators.

Automatic indexing programs appear, at least on the surface, to be perfectly suited for qualitative research purposes, but they do have their drawbacks, as the following example will suggest. One of the best-selling automatic indexers, ZyIndex, was used recently to index and search a huge collection of anthropological field data on folk concepts of purity and pollution in rural Orissa. The field notes were derived from on-the-scene tape recordings, which were then transcribed into the equivalent of roughly 4,000 pages of typed, double-spaced text. The resulting data base is stored on dozens of floppy disks; even so, virtually any paragraph within it is accessible in a matter of seconds via a key-word search. The major advantage of indexing material in this way is that it aids the memory, or so argues Alan Fiske, a lecturer and researcher in the university's Department of Behavioral Sciences. Under precomputer conditions, Fiske maintains, an ethnographer would gradually lose the recollection of many instances of a concept in the data base. ZyIndex's vast and seemingly unerring memory, however, makes it possible to retrieve "precisely the information we want for a particular study or project" (Zylab, 1985).

But are these retrieval operations really all that accurate? As anyone who has ever searched a textual data base with these techniques knows all too well, any search is likely to produce *false drops,* or retrieved records that contain one of the search words used only in a peripheral sense. For example, a search of the Orissa data base for traditional Hindu concepts of pollution might turn up a record in which an informant is complaining about air pollution from a factory. A false drop, in short, is not relevant to the search concept. The trouble is that, as research in information science has demonstrated, a search that aims for perfect *recall*—the retrieval of all relevant records from the data base—will have low *precision,* measured as the ratio between the number of relevant documents retrieved and the total number of records retrieved. To put it another way, a high-recall search is bound to produce a great many false drops, messing up the otherwise pristine picture of computer efficiency. What is more, aiming for high precision sacrifices recall—some relevant records will be missed.

This search technology, in short, is far from perfect, although a highly skilled searcher can learn to use the search question language to minimize the difficulties. Proximity operators, for instance, can be used to reduce the number of false drops. As Mr. Fiske explains, "We simply ask the computer to find either 'pollution within 10 words of caste' or 'pollution within 20 words of air'—this lets us zero in instantly on whichever form of pollution we want to review" (Zylab, 1985). What is not acknowledged here is that, conceivably, a Hindu informant could be talking about a caste fanatic, a person who might believe (as did Arumuka Navalar, a famous Hindu reformer from Sri Lanka) that an Untouchable's pollution is transmitted not only by touch but also by air. The apparently clever retrieval operation using proximity operators, in sum, shows precisely why it is said that precision and recall are inversely related: the retrieval operation seeks to maximize precision by reducing the number of false drops, but may well do so by missing some relevant documents. Computer-based retrieval techniques from textual data bases are, in short, inherently imperfect and should be viewed with some suspicion. And this point applies, it should be added, not only to automatic indexers, but more broadly, to all programs that use Boolean or proximity operators for data retrieval purposes.

Searches of textual data bases are inherently "fuzzy" in yet another way as well. On a fundamental level, such searches represent an attempt to retrieve *concepts* (such as *Hindu pollution*) through the use of an imperfect surrogate: words, or more precisely, strings. The problem here is that "a concept might be represented with many [different] words and a word can mean different things in different contexts" (Adams, 1979: 374). Arguably, a passage of text might well prove germane to a concept even though it does not mention the search string—or any of the synonyms that even a clever searcher might come up with. This point suggests even further grounds, in sum, for regarding the results of a retrieval operation with some suspicion. For any given search, there may well be additional relevant material in the data base that has not been retrieved, simply because the search question did not include the proper synonyms.

What we confront here, in part, is the discrepancy between the symbolic content of the computer (e.g., "precise," "unerring," and the like) and the reality of text-retrieval operations, which are inherently fuzzy and inaccurate. This software, in short, comes with a built-in dose of obfuscating ideology. That said, there are still ample grounds to argue that an automatic indexing storage and retrieval program has a fruitful role to play in the analysis of qualitative data—especially when its limitations are clearly understood and its role is put in its proper perspective. It is, after all, quite handy to be able to retrieve all, or almost all, instances of a given string in a huge textual data base.

Yet there is another danger lurking in the world of preunderstandings associated with this software. Automatic indexing programs are direct descendants of the software used on large, mainframe-based bibliographic retrieval systems, such as BRS Information Technologies or DIALOG Information services. These programs are, in other words, saturated with the values of their social origins within the related worlds of librarianship and information science. These values, although appropriate within the library world, are quite inappropriate for qualitative research applications.

From the information science standpoint, the material contained in a computer-based collection of field notes is *data,* viewed in the strict (and to me, strange) sense as "raw facts," which are inherently undifferentiated and unstructured. The first fundamental notion of information processing is that it is desirable to clear away all this clutter of data, producing out of it *information,* or "raw facts that have been turned into useful facts" (O'Leary and Williams, 1986: 61). The second fundamental notion of information processing is that the computer can do this more or less automatically, and that this is a good thing.

These notions make good sense for an inventory of automobile parts, and they might even make some sense for bibliographic retrieval operations, but they are wholly inapplicable to the analysis of qualitative data. In qualitative data, the *significant* patterns are not principally encoded in any form that the computer can detect, namely, in instances (or absences) of lexical items. Such patterns are, for one thing, conceptual rather than lexical, and it has already been demonstrated that retrieval operations only masquerade at the retrieval of concepts. What is more, it is a basic canon of qualitative data analysis that the meaningful patterns in the data emerge only after a deliberate (and human) confrontation with the data, in which the text is read, reread, and most importantly of all, *rewritten.* The rewriting process, in which the researcher reorganizes the material and amplifies it from memory, is crucial to the quality of the analysis.

What is so destructive about the information science preunderstanding of the "textual data base" is that it sees the text as a *fixed* entity, and what is more, an entity whose significant patterns can be divulged by automatic processing operations. This image, at least when applied to qualitative field notes, is false and should be consciously and sedulously resisted. Even if consciously resisted, however, the tendency to treat the field notes as a fixed "data base" is reinforced by the software itself: any changes or additions made to the field notes will not affect retrieval operations unless the entire field notes corpus is deliberately reindexed, an operation that can take hours to perform if the data base is large.

The automatic indexing approach has yet another disadvantage, and this one is perhaps the gravest. As Agar (1986) has observed, a prominent feature of qualitative data is that it occurs in segmentable, distinct units called strips. The essential feature of a strip is that it is a bounded phenomenon, its boundaries being demarcated by informants themselves or by the field researcher. Analysis, arguably, requires the retrieval of the entire strip, not just a portion of it. In analytic induction, for instance, each similarly coded strip is examined in its *entirety,* and must be so examined, since the researcher is looking for any and all features that are *always* present when the coded social behavior is present. The difficulty with some automatic indexing programs is that they do not retrieve strips. Instead, they retrieve paragraphs of text

*C
June 11, 1982
Nainativu, Sri Lanka
Nakapucanai Amman Temple
Verbatim Notes—No. 27.

(Standing out in front of temple, watching ferry boats arrive from the mainland—some Hindus coming even though the festival was cancelled)

(A Sinhalese family is getting out of the boat. They're going to the Buddhist dagoba first, and I'll follow)

(At the dagoba)
"For centuries Sinhalese people have been coming here to <Nagadipa> (note: <Nagadipa>/ <Nainativu> = Sinhalese vs. Tamil???) because this is one of three places Lord Buddha visited in Sri Lanka" (he's a Sinhalese businessman, he says)

(The bhikku comes out)
'I know there is trouble, but the Tamil people here know me. They are fine people and I do not fear to be here.'
*E

Figure 5. User-Defined Data Retrieval Unit in Automatic Indexing Program

divorced from their context. In essence, the program imposes its own artificial definition of the retrieval unit (the paragraph) on the data, obscuring from view the phenomenologically rich boundaries that are in themselves significant units of analysis. To be sure, the retrieved paragraphs could be used as a guide to a printed version of the data in its original integrity (or the original disk file). Yet it would be tedious to go from the screen to a printed volume. In any case, what is suspect here is the *appearance*—a false one, I would argue—that the program is retrieving significant units of data; what it retrieves are units of data that are being defined clandestinely by the computer and ripped out of their contexts. The appearance is powerful enough, perhaps, to hoodwink even an experienced fieldworker into thinking that what appears on the screen is significant data instead of disembodied and artificially biased.

One way out of this problem is to use software that is specifically designed to retrieve units of data whose boundaries are determined by the user, not the software. Some automatic indexing programs (such as

FYI 3000[1] and WordCruncher[2]) include optional modes in which the user can demarcate a unit of coherent data using special symbols (such as *C and *E) which the program then uses as a unit of retrieval (Figure 5). Other automatic indexers allow the user to browse through the files that are retrieved, thus enabling the analyst to see the significant boundaries in the data. A special-purpose program specifically designed for the retrieval of coded field notes, the ETHNOGRAPH (Seidel and Clark, 1984), appears to respect the integrity of the retrieved data.

Hypertext

The ultimate salvation of the text file approach to field notes, however, may depend on the creation and marketing of an entirely new kind of software, *hypertext* (Nelson, 1980). Hypertext software is now available in microcomputer formats.[3]

A hypertext program can be thought of, broadly, as a text-oriented data base management retrieval program, but one that augments computer search techniques based on Boolean or proximity operators. In addition to automated search procedures, hypertext software enables the user to go through the text manually, inserting invisible marks that link related units of text, as if an invisible thread were being tied between them. In this way, the user can create and save an "associative trail" through a complex and voluminous corpus of text. Suppose, for example, I realize while analyzing my field notes that the Sri Lankan pilgrimages, Nainativu and Kataragama, are in many respects polar opposites of one another. To explore this idea, I can search through the textual corpus, finding records that pertain in any way to Nainativu or Kataragama. As I do, and as I find units of text that highlight the comparison, I tag them. Since the program saves this trail, I can retrace my steps through the entire trail of associations I've created. In the end, hundreds of such trails will crisscross my notes, and I can recall any of them at a keystroke.

Hypertext software is obviously of great interest to qualitative researchers. The associative links one creates with hypertext can be subsumed under analytical categories, and the analytical categories can themselves be linked so that a complex and even hierarchical set of pathways through the text is established. Not all "hypertext" programs now available, to be sure, have such capabilities. Now that the hypertext concept has caught on, software companies are rehashing old products so that they appear to have hypertext capabilities, but such capabilities may well be minimal.

```
Date       |
Location   |
Topic      |
Note Type  |
Notes      |
```

Figure 6. Blank Form

Once these links have been created, the hypertext program allows the user to activate them by opening multiple windows on the screen. The user may thus "walk the paths" that have been deliberately created, adding to them and refining them as necessary. As the user performs this operation, Gerson (1987: 206) notes, analysis should proceed from "weakly structured text and naive analytical categories" to "highly structured text and more sophisticated categories"—which is, it should be noted, precisely the goal of qualitative data analysis.

Text-Oriented Data Base Management Programs

Text-oriented data base management programs such as Notebook II[4] resemble business data base management programs, but they are specifically designed for the storage and retrieval of large amounts of text. Such programs offer several significant advantages over the word processing text file/automatic indexing approach to the creation and analysis of field notes.

In common with business data base management programs, text-oriented data base managers allow the user to create a form for data entry (Figure 6), which consists of a series of *data fields* or spaces in which a certain kind of data may be entered. When the form is filled in, it is called a data record (Figure 7). Unlike most data base management programs, however, text-oriented programs allow the user to enter large amounts of text—as much as 30,000 characters—in each data field. To facilitate the entry and revision of text within the fields, the better text-oriented data base managers provide a variety of word processing functions, including the commands for block move operations that are so useful for text revision purposes. Virtually anything that can be placed in a word processing program's text file can be placed in a text-oriented data manager's form. Such programs therefore offer all the advantages of word processing for extensive revision, rewriting, and coding. Some of them, moreover, do not require an additional indexing operation to ensure accurate retrieval after changes are made to the data

Date	6-11-82
Location	Nainativu, Sri Lanka, Nakapucanai Amman Temple
Topic	Interethnic interaction at pilgrimage site
Note Type	Verbatim account
Notes	

(Standing out in front of temple, watching ferry boats arrive from the mainland—some Hindus coming even though the festival was cancelled)

(A Sinhalese family is getting out of the boat. They're going to the Buddhist dagoba first, and I'll follow)

(At the dagoba)
"For centuries Sinhalese people have been coming here to <Nagadipa> (note: <Nagadipa>/<Nainativu> = Sinhalese vs. Tamil???) because this is one of three places Lord Buddha visited in Sri Lanka" (he's a Sinhalese businessman, he says)

(The bhikku comes out)
'I know there is trouble, but the Tamil people here know me. They are fine people and I do not fear to be here.'

Figure 7. Data Record

records; thus there is no penalty attached to the frequent revision of notes.

Text-oriented data base managers are, arguably, at their best just where the text file/automatic indexer approach is weakest or suspect: in providing the right tools for data analysis. Unlike some automatic indexing programs, a text-oriented data base manager's standard unit of data storage and retrieval is not the paragraph, but the data record, which—so long as the form is well designed—should correspond to a single strip. In other words, text-oriented data base managers can be thought of as programs for creating, storing, searching, sorting, and grouping phenomenologically valid units of data. Specifically, they provide the following procedures for data maintenance and analysis:

— *Sorting* the data records in numerical order or alphabetical order. Sorts can occur on any field. In the examples shown in Figures 6 and 7, for instance, the data base could be sorted chronologically by **date,** geographically by **location,** substantively by **topic,** or typologically by the type of field notes recorded (by **note type**). Some programs allow multiple sorts, in which the data base is sorted initially by one field (such as **date**) and subsequently by a second field (such as **topic**). The second sort resolves records left unordered by the first one. Assume, for instance, that the first sort occurs on the field **date** and the second on the field **topic**. If there are several records for 6-11-82, these records will be organized alphabetically by topic.

— *Finding* a form that contains a particular word or words. Available with most programs are sophisticated search tools, such as Boolean operators, truncation, and wild card characters.

— *Grouping* related forms together into a subunit of the data base called a *view*. This operation is also called *selection*. Of obvious value for analytic induction and constant comparison, this function permits the user to form a view, for instance, of all the records in which the field **topic** contains "interethnic interaction at pilgrimage sites." As new notes are being recorded and coding occurs, all previous instances of the use of a code can be quickly reviewed by forming a view of, for instance, all the records in which the field **codes** contain "ethnic interaction."

Such operations have obvious value for the field analysis techniques developed by qualitative researchers.

Text-oriented data managers do have their drawbacks for qualitative research purposes. The first and most vexing drawback is that the data must be contained in a single file, which in a qualitative research setting is likely to outgrow the confines of a floppy disk in short order. The use of such software for field note purposes will invariably require a high capacity floppy drive (1.2 megabytes or more) or, better, a 10 to 20 megabyte hard disk drive. However, such drives are becoming increasingly common, even in portable computers.

The second drawback concerns data security. Hard disks occasionally fail, resulting in the destruction of all the information stored on them. The use of a hard disk therefore requires the regular transfer of the stored data to backup media, such as a streaming tape drive, which adds considerably to the cost of the computer system. A sensible alternative is to use archival programs that allow large hard disk files to be backed up on a series of floppy disks.

The third drawback concerns the technique used to perform searching, sorting, and grouping operations in the data base. Unlike automatic indexing programs, which create an inverted file index and search the index instead of the actual data base, many text-oriented data base managers perform sequential searches in the manner of a word processing program. Such searches are advantageous in that it is not necessary to reindex the data base every time a record is altered. Were they to proceed too slowly, however, they could frustrate data analysis by imposing tedious waits on the researcher who wishes to sort or group records. The best text-oriented data base managers, however, use sophisticated algorithms to perform these functions, and perform at acceptable levels. Notebook II, for example, sorts or groups some 90 records in a 525K data base, one containing nearly one-half million characters of text, in 30 seconds.

A fourth drawback is that most data base management programs impose severe penalties on the user who wishes to change the arrangement of headings or data fields in the form—indeed, some programs do not allow any changes to be made at all. A researcher who realizes that a form has been improperly designed may be in for some trouble if a large quantity of data has already been entered. Anyone contemplating the use of such programs should make sure, therefore, that changes to the form are possible without requiring hand reentry of the data.

A word of caution. Before committing large amounts of time and work to typing data into a data base managment program, make sure the data base design is adequate for its intended purpose. Many field researchers have typed in huge amounts of data to such programs, only to find later that the data base design is inadequate for data retrieval and analysis. Many programs do not permit changes after data have been entered, and those that do place limits on the scope of reorganization that is possible. Get help designing the form you will use to hold records and, before committing yourself to its use, test it out on five or ten records of data. You will doubtless find that the form needs alteration.

Concordance Generation Software

The late British anthropologist E. E. Evans-Pritchard liked to say that a penetrating analysis of a culture often has its start in the researcher's growing grasp of a few, key terms. A *concordance generation program* can play a major role in the growth of this kind of understanding.

Concordance generation programs were initially devised to create concordances of literary texts. A *concordance* is a reference work that lists in alphabetical order each word used in the text, showing its location (by page number and paragraph) in a standard version of the literary work. A *key-word-in-context* (KWIC) concordance shows the words with their surrounding context (Figure 8), which is often defined

		asked	(6)
1:2	After he had eaten she	asked	him to go to the river
1:2	thirst. But the old man	asked	her to accompany him to which
1:2	to her his love and	asked	her to become his wife.
2:1	Ganesha, whom Skanda had	asked	to hide himself in the
2:1	girl, frightened to death,	asked	for the old man's protection
2:2	herself at his feet and	asked	his pardon, as she had at

Figure 8. Part of a Key-Word-In-Context (KWIC) Concordance

arbitrarily as the 40 or 50 characters to the left and right of the word as it appears in the original text. The creation of a concordance by hand would, obviously, take a great deal of time and expense, even for a short text. Now that concordance generation programs are available for microcomputers,[5] however, concordances can be produced at low cost and their use is becoming increasingly common in literary analysis. Concordances are frequently used to discover how a particular author uses a given word, and the results can prove illuminating (Burton, 1980, 1981a, 1981b, 1982; Feldman and Norman, 1987; Hockey, 1980; Preston and Coleman, 1978).

Computer-generated concordances are frequently criticized for determining the context arbitrarily (Burton, 1982). In Figure 8, for example, from three to five words to the left or right of the key word are shown. The context is often unclear. The usefulness of concordances is greatly increased when an entire sentence (not just a few words to the left and right of the word) is retrieved and printed, but few concordance programs make this option available.

The use of concordances has spread beyond the confines of literary criticism, and concordance generation is becoming a standard tool of research in political science. Many studies have been made, for instance, of how politicians use words in political speeches. In the 1980 election, for example, a concordance of the word *rights* (Weber, 1984: 131) suggests that when the Republicans used the word, the rights they had in mind were those (inter alia) of law-abiding citizens, state and local authorities, parents, women (but always with the admonition that the ERA is not needed), and would-be Soviet emigrants. When the Democrats used the word, however, they were thinking of the rights of working women, minority women, striking workers, pregnant women, industrial laborers, farm laborers, the disabled, the victims of civil rights violations, and black South Africans. It could well be argued that one does not need a computer to tell the difference between the Republican and Democratic party platforms in 1980. To be fair, however, it should be noted that this example draws on a much-discussed public issue. An analysis of this sort could prove illuminating, at least in an introductory sense, when the two parties are not so familiar and their rhetoric has not been so extensively analyzed.

As this example shows, concordances are frequently used to illuminate differences between two texts, or alternatively, to clarify the distinctive way that a particular text uses the language (measured against an implicit or explicit norm of language usage). According to the advocates of such uses, the computer produces "objective" data demonstrating that such differences or distinctive patterns indeed exist. Some substantial theoretical and methodological problems lurk beneath the surface of such uses, however, and not all qualitative researchers will commend the way that political sociologists and literary critics have tried to resolve them. Chapter 4 returns to this issue in more detail.

There is a way, though, that concordances can be worked into a qualitative research program without raising these issues—and, what is more, in a way that enhances the recursive, discover-as-you-go quality of qualitative research. This approach (like the others discussed in this chapter) insists that data analysis is not something that happens after field research is over; it should occur in the field and during the research. Here is a brief overview of one such strategy.

Whenever notes are being entered into the field note corpus that contain an informant's statements or responses to an interview question, the researcher uses the program's copy-and-write command to copy such statements or responses to a separate text file. This text file contains nothing but the language encountered in the field. Periodically, the researcher runs the concordance program on this text file, and sits down to read it, looking deliberately for exophora (see previous mention) that appear incoherent. Such a strategy amounts, in effect, to a deliberate search for what Agar calls breakdowns. Such searches for incoherent exophora should prove useful in contributing to the growing grasp of native terms that Evans-Pritchard commended. In particular, when a researcher finds that a word is unintelligible in its context, further research and inquiry are mandated to uncover and understand the cultural knowledge needed to interpret the use of the word correctly.

Some researchers may be tempted to try to produce an after-the-field concordance of their entire field note corpus, and the idea has some appeal. But be forewarned. A concordance of a 100,000 word text—a fairly short one—required 1,458 pages of printout (Feldman and

Norman, 1987: 84). At this rate, 5,000 pages of field research data could generate an 18,000 page concordance! Obviously, concordance generation software is best used for focused studies of smaller texts.

Idea Processing Software

The final step in the analysis of field notes occurs when the researcher reorganizes them for rhetorical purposes, that is, for presentation as evidence in an essay or book. And here it is especially important not to be hoodwinked by the notion of the field notes as an authoritative, sacrosanct "data base," the structure and contents of which are fixed and eternal. In fact, the text contained in any data base of field notes is malleable and able to be copied, and can be freely passed from one program to the next. The more clearly this point is understood, the more potential there is that writing up the results of the research can itself provide a fruitful context for further data analysis and theoretical discovery.

Research on the composition process has revealed that writing is itself a form of thinking and discovery (Rohman, 1965; Flower and Hayes, 1980). As writers develop their ideas, they cycle recursively among three distinct phases of the composition process, which Flower and Hayes (1981) call *planning, translating,* and *reviewing.* A writer begins with a plan, tries to translate it into written form, reviews it and finds it unsatisfactory, revises the plan, and so on. The process continues recursively until the writer is satisfied with the results.

Writing up the results of qualitative research requires yet another element in this recursive process: entering into a dialogue with an immense amount of textual data. The richness and texture of qualitative research reports is highly dependent on how well the writer incorporates data access strategies into the writing process. This fact, coupled with the malleability and copiability of the stored data, suggests the enormous promise of a two-pronged approach to rhetorical reorganization using a *memory-resident idea processing program.*

Idea processing programs such as ThinkTank help writers create outlines using a nested, hierarchical structure. They do so by providing special commands that facilitate the creation and reorganization of such outlines. So that the writer can see the overall structure of a large outline, subordinate headings can be hidden or collapsed so that only the first-level, main headings remain visible. The reverse process, expansion, reveals headings that have been hidden in this way. Other commands permit the user to restructure the outline; headings at any level can be moved up or down in the outline, or left or right (thus increasing or diminishing their importance). All restructuring operations result in automatic renumberings of the headings and subheadings. Unlimited amounts of text, moreover, can be stored in collapsed or hidden form under headings at any level of the outline.

Idea processing programs, in short, provide an ideal way of developing an argument and of organizing huge amounts of text that will be used to support the argument. Until memory-resident idea processors[6] came along, however, the process of moving textual data into the idea processing program imposed time penalties on this promising process. A memory-resident program takes advantage of the large amounts of internal memory available with today's microcomputers. With such programs, it is possible to load two or more application programs into the computer's memory at one time, and to move from one to the next with a keystroke. What is more, some memory-resident programs provide tools to move text from one program to another in just a few keystrokes. A qualitative researcher can use this technology to achieve major gains in the accessibility and transferability of huge amounts of textual data. The key is to load the field notes data base (using an automatic indexer or a text-oriented data manager) and then, on top of it, a memory-resident idea processor.

With both programs in memory, the writer can develop a rhetorical strategy by cycling back and forth between the data itself (stored in the data base) and the emerging writing plan (captured in the idea processor's outline form). Using the data retrieval program, the writer can quickly locate material in the data base and review it. Text that appears to be worth citing in the research report can be easily and quickly moved from the data record to the outline and captured as a textual entry beneath the headings. And as the outline begins to take form, restructuring operations will automatically move this text along with the headings, so that even a massive amount of textual material can be quickly and easily reordered. Once all the material in the data base has been reviewed in this way, and pasted into the outline where appropriate, the finished outline can be printed to a text file and taken up by a word processing program.

4. AUTOMATIC DATA ANALYSIS

The storage, retrieval, and analysis strategies discussed in Chapter 3 share one element in common: they are designed to automate purely perfunctory tasks, such as sorting, finding, retrieving, and reorganizing the mass of qualitative data, so that the researcher can proceed with data analysis. The analysis itself, however, is still an entirely human affair; the computer aids it by making the field notes available (as Ada Augusta would say), but the computer does not perform any data analysis itself. Discussed in this chapter, however, are approaches in which the computer performs the analysis automatically. It begins with a critical analysis of computer-based *content analysis,* or the use of such techniques as word frequency analysis and content category dictionaries to make inferences from documents (Weber, 1984), such as interview transcriptions, autobiographies, life histories, speeches, or transcriptions of folktales. Also discussed are data base management approaches to what Smith (1982) calls *enumerative induction,* the quantitative analysis of observed qualitative phenomena.

Word Frequency Analysis

A word frequency list, a list of how many times a given word occurs in a text (Figure 9), can be compiled with a microcomputer's aid. The text is a Tamil folktale from Sri Lanka. (Note: Words that appear only once in the text are omitted from the figure.) With a computer, the procedure is effortless. What is substantially less easy is to decide what the compiled data means, and how reliable one's interpretations of it can be.

What does a word frequency list tell us? In literary analysis, one frequently cited purpose of compiling a word frequency list is to determine what Baudelaire called the "obsession" of a writer—the subject that is closest to the writer's heart and purpose (Feldman and Norman, 1987: 92). Literary studies have indeed shown that every writer has a distinctive and characteristic vocabulary. This characteristic vocabulary is typified by a word frequency configuration that is significantly different (in the quantitative sense) from the normal frequencies of word usage. Such usage norms are determined by word frequency analyses of large amounts of contemporary language use (Kenny, 1982). When an author departs significantly from usage norms, one could argue persuasively that his or her characteristic "obsession" is revealed. Most literary studies that have used word frequency analysis,

```
**********   Unique Words Read  =                    197
**********   Total Words Read   =                    429
**********   Total Chars Read   =                   1857
        7 skanda
        6 asked
        6 valliyamma
        5 man
        4 jungle
        4 old
        4 wife
        3 cave
        3 decided
        3 found
        3 into
        3 kataragama
        3 so
        2 become
        2 called
        2 day
        2 did
        2 elephant
        2 eventually
        2 go
        2 himself
        2 however
        2 killed
        2 leave
        2 love
        2 once
        2 short
        2 took
        2 up
        2 valli
        2 vedda
        2 veddas
        2 wild
        2 yams
        2 young
```

Figure 9. Word Frequency List (Sorted by Frequency)

however, have been concerned with cases of disputed authorship; the true author is revealed by his or her linguisic "fingerprint."

Word frequency lists can prove useful even when usage norms are absent: If every author's linguistic fingerprint is unique, it follows that each fingerprint will differ from another author's fingerprint just as it differs from the norm. Mosteller and Wallace (1964) used precisely this assumption to determine the authorship of some of the unsigned Federalist papers.

Can these techniques be applied to social science? Political sociologists use word frequency lists to determine the "obsession," not of an author, but of a political speaker, and the comparison drawn is not to the norm for the language but the word choices of a political opponent (Weber, 1984: 129-130). In the 1980 elections, for instance, the words *Soviet, military,* and *defense* ranked high in Reagan's list, but did not make the top 25 most frequently used words in Carter's. Carter was concerned with such matters as health and education, which escape mention in Reagan's list of high frequency words. A variant of this comparative approach is to compare the same party's platform over time (e.g., Johnson, 1979).

As this example suggests, sociological applications of word frequency analysis make an assumption, namely, that the gross frequency of *surface* linguistic phenomena—the words in a text—provides a more or less sound index of *themes* of some sort, themes that go beyond the text itself and tell us something about the social world from which it was drawn. On the macroanalytic level, such themes are said to be *culture indicators,* which inform the researcher about the "state of beliefs, values, ideologies, or other cultural systems" in a particular place at a particular time (Weber, 1984: 127; see also Klingemann et al., 1982; Namenwirth, 1969, 1973, 1983; Namenwirth and Laswell, 1970; Rosengren, 1981; and Weber, 1983). Such studies have been applied to micro-level social analyses as well, using such texts as small group discussions, letters, diaries, song lyrics of a subculture, suicide notes, and myths (Aries, 1977; Namenwirth, 1969a, 1970; Walker, 1975; Weber, 1984). The advocates of word frequency and other content analyses sometimes insist, in fact, that such themes as these are best discovered through the quantitative study of words, because such studies are unobstrusive and quantitative (e.g., Lasswell, 1965).

What makes the critics of word frequency analysis uncomfortable is the simplistic—indeed, naive—assumption that the gross, surface phenomena of the text (word frequencies) are reliable indicators of its social and cultural context. This assumption is fraught with difficulties. It is inadmissible for any word that can be used in multiple senses, for example, such as *play* (Dunphy, 1966). Since many words have multiple meanings, it is arguable that no word frequency analysis will mean much unless all the words in the text are "disambiguated" by means of a tedious, manual coding scheme. So much for the putative advantages of automatic processing!

The problems of word frequency analysis, however, go further than this, and deserve close attention. Consider, for instance, a study that seeks to compare management and employee attitudes about productivity. Transcriptions of extensive interviews, suitably disambiguated, are subjected to word frequency analysis, and it turns out that no significant difference can be found in the frequencies of employee and management use of the word "productivity." One could conclude that both the management and the employees are expressing an "obsession" with productivity, and that the frequency with which this word is used testifies to a company-wide concern with levels of production. On closer inspection of the texts in question, however, it turns out that employees are making statements such as:

> Productivity, productivity, productivity. All they care about is our damned productivity—get the stuff out the door. They don't give a damn about the things we care about, and I can tell you this much, productivity ain't one of them.

This example is of course contrived. Yet it points to a fundamental interpretive problem with the assumptions underlying word frequency analysis: it ignores the *communicative intent* of word usage and confuses the *frequency* of a word's usage with *importance* as a valid theme of the speaker's culture (see also Krippendorf, 1980; Chomsky, 1959). In this example, the word "productivity" is repeated to lampoon the way management nags workers to work harder, and the informant specifically states that productivity is *not* a theme of the workers' subculture. Word frequency analysis, in short, tempts one to make unwarranted and simplistic assumptions about the speaker's or writer's motives in using a word or words (Altheide, 1987). It is completely insensitive to such common linguistic phenomena such as negation and irony (Krippendorf, 1980: 162), and submerges situational or contextual information in a way that can prove misleading. Altheide and Snow (1979), for instance, argue that events with certain characteristics (accessibility, visual quality, drama, and action) are likely to be selected for TV news coverage *because* they can be readily shaped to the network news format, not because network executives or advertisers are particularly inclined to emphasize certain themes.

To be sure, the assumption that word frequencies represent the existence of themes in a text may actually prove valid in certain contexts—political speeches, for instance, in which the communicator is making a deliberate effort to emphasize precisely those themes that will bring in the votes. Political rhetoric tries to make themes explicit—perhaps that is why most successful content analyses use political texts, such as speeches and propaganda. Yet in the kind of natural, situation-based social interaction most frequently observed by qualitative social scientists, informants may not often use words that are explicitly linked to the themes that are truly significant in their social life. We recognize this fact when we say, "It goes without saying," or "I didn't realize for a year that what they were *really* saying to me was, 'If you want to get ahead in this company, don't rock the boat. We're pretty happy with the way things are right now'."

Much of what a qualitative researcher seeks to grasp "goes without saying" in precisely this way, and it has to be uncovered by paying attention to the tacit dimension of social life—what the philosopher Alfred Schutz calls the common-sense, taken-for-granted world of everyday reality (Schutz, 1967). It is precisely because such themes are taken for granted that people do not talk about them much. A case in point: Pool (1952) observes that words pertaining to democracy do not appear frequently when democracy is accepted and functioning well; it is when democratic procedures and institutions are in dispute that usage frequencies rise. If such themes are referred to at all, the references may well be oblique or expressed using paralinguistic phenomena such as kinesics. We're back, in other words, in the world of exophora, and the only way to cope with this unknown world is by going beyond the gross, surface appearance of social reality and filling in the missing knowledge. In conclusion, then, word frequency lists are best applied to texts that are *intended in some way to make cultural themes explicit,* such as suicide notes, political speeches, political songs, propaganda, or auto-biographies; they would be misused, arguably, where such intentions are absent.

Content Category Analysis

Even in cases in which assumptions about a speaker's or writer's intentions are warranted, word frequency analyses have a major disadvantage. By disaggregating words into a simple list that is sorted alphabetically or by frequency, such analyses may obscure themes that speakers or writers express using a variety of words. A concern for wealth, for example, could well be expressed using not just one word, such as *money,* but a wide variety of them, including *abundance, affluence, bonus, capital, commerce, dollar, economy, employment, enterprise, estate, goods, incentive, income, luxury, price, property, prosperity, salary, wage,* and *worth.* Arguably, a text that shows a concern for wealth would use this category of words more frequently than a text that does not.

Recognition of this point has led to the widespread use of *content category dictionaries* in content analysis. A content category dictionary is an exhaustive list of all the words that can conceivably be linked to a theme of some sort, such as "well-being," "deprivation," or "anxiety." The categories are called *tags,* and processing involves tagging the words and counting up the instances of each tag. The use of such content category dictionaries is claimed to resolve some of the shortcomings of word frequency analyses. The use of a cluster of words (rather than just one), for instance, may reduce problems of word ambiguity; if the speaker's concern is with poverty, for example, this theme will come out even if the contrasting word "rich" sometimes appears in the text ("I stepped out of my poor, tumbledown shack, and a rich stench struck my nostrils from the garbage dump"). The use of such dictionaries cannot overcome the problems induced by assuming the speaker's intention to highlight themes, however, so this kind of content analysis is still best applied to texts that seek to make themes explicit.

A researcher can create a content category dictionary or use one of the several that have already been compiled (e.g., Kelly and Stone, 1975; Laswell and Namenwirth, 1968). Easily created by the researcher, the simplest dictionaries comprise just a few tags and short word lists. Simple dictionaries have a major advantage: they force the researcher to focus on developing an explicit rationale for the inclusion of every tag and every word in the dictionary. Such a rationale is vital for, as Krippendorf (1980: 40-42) emphasizes, a content category dictionary amounts to a hypothesis that the words it contains are valid indexes of some social or psychological state. Yet many content analysis studies rely on the published dictionaries—and for the simple reason of practicality. Such dictionaries provide a "standardized classification instrument," facilitating comparison from study to study regardless of social context, and they "minimize the time needed for dictionary construction, validation, and revision" (Brent, 1984: 132). The Lasswell Value Dictionary (LVD), the largest of such instruments, occupies three published volumes and is available in computer-readable form (Stone et al., 1966).

Most qualitative researchers will have no quarrel with the context-sensitive dictionaries that a fieldworker creates, save that the standard procedures of content analysis are overly linear and nonrecursive (more on that point anon). The use of prepackaged, computer-readable dictionaries, however, raises serious issues of theory and method. Each such dictionary contains a plethora of covert theoretical assumptions. In LVD, for example, the tag WEALTH-OTHER, for instance, subsumes words (other than those pertaining to economic transactions and roles) that are assumed to *index* the importance of economic concerns in the text under analysis. The problem is that the words so subsumed are drawn from a culturally and temporally specific universe of discourse, namely, American political rhetoric of the 1940s and 1950s. In such rhetoric, for example, the theme of wealth is expressed using such words as *bargain, corn, balance of trade, inventory, tin* and *unemployment index.* Arguably, problems will arise when this dictionary is used outside the temporal circumstances of its creation; WEALTH-OTHER list probably does not contain all the terms needed, for instance, a concern for wealth in today's American political rhetoric (consider *foreign competition, dumping,* and *microchip*). For non-Western cultures, such lists are close to useless. The Vellalar agriculturalists of northern Sri Lanka, for instance, do not use these words when they are talking about wealth. Instead, they use terms such as *increase, gold, the waxing moon, auspicious, new rice, the god Pillaiyar,* and *the goddess Lakshmi.* One does not have to go to a non-Western cultural setting, moreover, to find unfamiliar ways of expressing a theme with a unique discovery; as Sykes (1977: 408) and other investigators of police behavior have observed, police develop an "argot" to describe their activities, and this language can and should be developed into a category system for analytic purposes.

This point suggests that the construction of a culturally specific and culturally valid content category dictionary could well prove to be a significant mode of qualitative investigation in itself, and as it is being created and successively refined, it could be used recursively on field-derived texts to see whether it is succeeding in capturing the themes the field researcher sees. Yet the research values associated with the content analysis tradition place little emphasis on this point. Content analysis textbooks do not emphasize recursive processes of discovery. On the contrary, they emphasize practicality, expense reduction, and a linear, positivistic model of research, in which one starts with a theory ("operationalized" as a content category dictionary), obtains the sample, performs the computations, and assesses the results.

That such a design would be recommended is hardly surprising. Academic reputations and careers, for instance, are furthered by making the claim that one's activities are "scientific," and the use of the computer adds symbolic weight to the claim. And, to be sure, there are good grounds for claiming that the abuses and excesses of content analysis in the past require concern for such matters as sampling, reliability, and validity; the approach now advocated takes the researcher (as well as his or her biases) out of the research setting, substituting instead a set of rigorous and highly quantitative procedures for assessing such matters as intercoder reliability. The goal throughout is to use a cost-effective and highly unobtrusive measure that gets the job done as fast (and as reliably) as possible. Yet the persistent disinterest in the building of content category dictionaries as a form of cultural discovery has at least some of its roots, arguably, in the social circumstances in which computer-based content analysis arose.

Until recently, the software required to perform a content analysis using a content category dictionary could be used only on mainframe computers. What is more, the chief proponents of content analysis developed their techniques back in the days when computer input required the use of punched cards. Both of these factors contributed to the way content analysis has been conceived. Most researchers had to pay for mainframe time, so a premium was placed on quick, one-shot analyses. To do the analysis over again would be too expensive; all the effort was placed on getting it right the first time. The fact that all the data had to be input on punched cards only added to the high cost of repeated analyses. Under such circumstances, no one in his or her right mind would have viewed a content category study as a technique suitable for recursive, reflexive, and reiterative data exploration.

With the advent of interactive microcomputers and good content analysis software for them, however, the door has been thrown open to a new kind of recursive, qualitative content analysis, one that views the creation of a content category dictionary as something of an end in itself. Since data entry is now possible with the keyboard and researchers now own microcomputers outright, there is no longer any penalty to repeated iterations of the analysis. A completely new strategy of content analysis therefore becomes possible: The researcher goes from text to dictionary and back again, refining the categories and testing the dictionary's usefulness in constant confrontation with the textual data. Through this recursive process, the researcher's grasp of the text is successively modeled in the structure and vocabulary of the dictionary. Here there is little question of performing a quantitative analysis that "verifies" a "hypothesis"; the emphasis is not on the final product, but on the process of discovery that these techniques can and should entail. This form of qualitative content analysis (compare Altheide, 1987) puts the researcher back into the research process, places emphasis on critical reflection, and rejects the linear, hypothetico-deductive model of positivistic research; it substitutes in its place a hermeneutic spiral of growing awareness. In this spiral, the initial dictionary generates problems when it is first used on a text. Resolving the problems by updating the dictionary leads to new awareness, new discoveries, and new knowledge; the new knowledge in turn mandates further updates and corrections to the dictionary, and so on (Lindkvist, 1981).

Enumerative Induction

Despite the strident tone of debate between advocates of quantitative and qualitative social science, the simple fact remains that qualities can be counted—and what is more, there is no necessary contradiction between the two strategies. Several authors speak of the fruitful interplay, for instance, between qualitative techniques and quantitative survey research; the one informs the other (e.g., Fielding and Fielding, 1986: 27). Increasing attention is being focused, too, on what Smith (1982) calls enumerative induction, the counting of observed qualities and the use of such counts in an overall program of qualitative research. As will be seen, microcomputer data base management programs provide fruitful tools for enumerative induction applications.

Qualitative researchers frequently observe behaviors that can be counted, and to facilitate such counts, they create observation and interview schedules such as the ones shown in Figures 10 and 11. Computer versions of these schedules can be created in a matter of minutes with a data base management program such as dBASE III, which is normally used for business applications. Figure 10 shows an observation schedule used to record phenomena connected with spirit possession trances in a Tamil village; Figure 11 shows an interview schedule devised for a household survey of pilgrimage behavior. Note that both schedules could have been created only after some immersion in the field research data. Both make use of indigenous terms and

1. Record no: _____
2. Sex: male [ ] female [ ]
3. Apparent age: child [ ] teenager [ ] young adult [ ]
                 mature adult [ ] elderly [ ]
4. Caste: _____
5. Dress: village/poor [ ] village/middling [ ]
          village/wealthy [ ] Western [ ]
6. Possession site: _____
7. Possession situation:
     kavati festival in village [ ]
     temple festival [ ]
     household shrine [ ]
     pucari's shrine [ ]

8. Possession features:
     glossolalia [ ]
     hyperventilation [ ]
     rolling around on ground [ ]
     exposure of genitals [ ]
     striking another person [ ]
        persons struck (and relationship): _____

     demand issued by possessing spirit [ ]
        describe: _____

     offering made to possessing spirit [ ]
        describe: _____

8. Possessing spirit or deity _____
       [. . .]
12. Duration of possession: short [ ] medium [ ] long [ ]

Figure 10. Observation Schedule for Spirit Possession Trances in a Tamil Village

include items that would be recognized by people familiar with the culture (but missed by outsiders). Note, too, that the use of such schedules mandates a search, not for quantities, but for the *presence* or *absence* of behaviors or attributes; items that could be quantified, such as "apparent age" in Figure 10, are converted into categories for analytical purposes. Such categories should be culturally meaningful.

The advantage of using data base management techniques for such

1. Head of household _____
2. Stage of household process:
   [ ] Inception—young couple alone or w/small children
   [ ] Mature—parents or other elders living in house

3. Description of house:

   Poor:
   [ ] Thatched mud, no compound
   [ ] Thatched mud, with compound

   Middling:
   [ ] Concrete with thatched roof
   [ ] Concrete with tile roof

   Wealthy:
   [ ] Large concrete house with tile roof & furniture
   [ ] One of the nicest houses in the village

4. Occupation (head of household):

   [ ] Agriculture (amount of rice land [ ]   dry land [ ])
   [ ] Caste-related occupation
   [ ] Trader
   [ ] Fisherman
   [ ] Government servant
   [ ] Industrial worker

        [. . .]

24. Pilgrimages undertaken in the past 5 years:

		Visits			Purpose	
		Frequent	Occ.	Seldom	Cumma	Nettikatan
[ ]	Celvacannati	[ ]	[ ]	[ ]	[ ]	[ ]
[ ]	Chidambaram	[ ]	[ ]	[ ]	[ ]	[ ]
[ ]	Kataragama	[ ]	[ ]	[ ]	[ ]	[ ]
[ ]	Maviddapuram	[ ]	[ ]	[ ]	[ ]	[ ]
[ ]	Nallur	[ ]	[ ]	[ ]	[ ]	[ ]
[ ]	Nainativu	[ ]	[ ]	[ ]	[ ]	[ ]

Figure 11. Interview Schedule

purposes is that these programs make it exceptionally easy to analyze the recorded data. The form of analysis, it should be understood, is not strictly or even predominantly quantitative; on the contrary, it is *logical,* in that it is concerned with the presence or absence of attributes, as well as with the texture of associations that such presences and absences create. The *query language* of such programs, the language used to ask questions of the data base, provides precisely the tools needed to reveal these textures (and to quantify the results). Such languages make possible an interactive, discovery-producing exploration of the stored data.

Consider, for instance, the following queries for the data base created by many recorded observations of spirit possessions:

— Do males voice demands issued by the possessing spirit more frequently (or less frequently) than females?
— Of the persons possessed by Virabattiran, what percent are dressed in village/poor or village/middling clothes?
— Do Nalavars engage in glossolalia more frequently than Vellalars?
— Do people with wealthy homes visit temples cumma (as tourists) more frequently than people with poor homes? Which caste visits temples most frequently to perform nerttikatan (vow fulfillment)?

Consider, too, the following queries of the data base generated by the household survey of pilgrimage behavior:

— Do Vellalars visit Maviddapuram more frequently than Nalavars?
— Which pilgrimage site is most popular among wealthy villagers? Poor? Middling? Which pilgrimage site is most popular among Nalavars?
— Which pilgrimage site is least popular among all pilgrims?
— Which pilgrimage sites do government servants prefer? Industrial workers?

As can be seen, the use of a query language on a data base of observation or interview schedules can uncover associations and patterns in the data that may not have been obvious to the researcher. The resulting discoveries can generate new hypotheses for research. However, it is usually difficult (and sometimes impossible) to change the data form once it has been created and used to fill in dozens or hundreds of records. The better programs for this application will provide accessible tools for such changes.

5. KNOWLEDGE-BASED STRATEGIES

Most of the newest (and noisiest) directions in qualitative computing involve the use of artificial intelligence (AI) programs and programming languages. AI is concerned, broadly, with the design of intelligent computer systems, which exhibit some of the characteristics associated with intelligence in human behavior, such as the ability to understand natural language, to reason, and to solve problems (Barr and Feigenbaum, 1981: 3). AI software, or so claim its proponents, differs radically from the programs discussed in previous chapters of this book. Non-AI software represents data and performs simple processing operations on it, such as sorting, counting, and searching. AI software, in contrast, represents knowledge and performs operations on it that are claimed to resemble the attributes of human intelligence, such as the use of logical deduction and heuristic strategies to solve problems.

Taking this claim at face value, then, these new approaches in qualitative computing can be called *knowledge-based strategies.* They are concerned with the representation, not of textual data, but of knowledge, and with applying knowledge-processing capabilities to qualitative research. The first applications of such software improved the performance of text searching. Such applications have found their way to qualitative computing and, when they become available for microcomputers, they may improve the performance of text-retrieval software (see, e.g., Shelly and Sibert, 1986). AI activity today, however, is dominated by the growing commercial and research use of *expert systems,* computer programs that are capable of simulating the expertise of a trained human professional in some limited domain of activity.

This chapter is devoted to analyzing the prospects of expert systems for qualitative computing applications, and for two reasons: expert systems are widely thought to represent AI's first major achievement and, what is more, expert system programming languages (such as PROLOG) and system development shells are widely available in microcomputer formats. There is every reason to suspect that qualitative researchers will make increasing use of these tools. What is far from clear, however, is whether such tools are actually useful for qualitative research applications. As will be seen, expert system software is deeply imbued with some potent preunderstandings, and a grasp of just how these programs could be used depends on how clearly qualitative researchers perceive these preunderstandings and clear them away.

Expert Systems

Early attempts to create computer programs with intelligent attributes focused on general problem-solving capabilities, but these efforts proved virtually fruitless. One conclusion soon emerged from such efforts: General problem-solving strategies probably do not exist. It was then hypothesized that problem-solving strategies are actually tied to specific knowledge domains, and are learned—and expressed—along with domain-specific facts and heuristic rules. If this assumption is correct, the key to creating an "intelligent" computer program is to limit it to a highly specialized domain of human expertise and represent that knowledge in a form the computer can process (Hayes-Roth et al., 1983; Waterman, 1986). This strategy led to the first major breakthrough of AI, the creation of *knowledge-based systems,* or, as they are more commonly known, *expert systems.* The term *expert system* has become widely accepted because most such systems are designed to simulate the performance of a highly trained human expert.

The programming languages from which programmers create expert systems are *declarative* rather than *procedural.* Statements in such languages, in other words, *declare* propositions about the world (i.e., *facts*) that give the computer procedures to follow. In PROLOG (Clocksin and Mellish, 1984), for example, one can declare such propositions in the following form:

likes(joe,mary)

which means "Joe likes Mary." One can create a data base of such propositions or facts:

likes(joe,mary)
likes(mary,steve)
likes(steve,mary)

Once such a data base of facts has been created, the program's *inference engine* can "read" it and answer the user's questions about the data base. *Inference engines,* in contrast to data retrieval programs, do not retrieve data to answer the user's question; in contrast, they deduce an answer (if possible) from the propositions the data base contains. Were the user to ask the inference engine, in effect, "Does Mary like Joe?" the answer would be "false." [This answer does not necessarily mean that Mary dislikes Joe; it means simply that there is no information in the data base of the form

likes(mary, joe).]

Now suppose one would like to ask, "Do Joe and Mary like each other?" The inference engine cannot deduce the answer to this question until a rule is added to the data base. Such a rule would provide the inference engine with a heuristic problem-solving strategy for determining whether two people like each other. Such a rule, in PROLOG, is as follows:

```
like_each_other :-
    likes(X,Y)
    likes(Y,X)
```

which reads, in effect, "Two people like each other IF person X likes person Y AND person Y likes person X." A data base created with PROLOG or other AI tools, then, consists of facts and rules, and the program's inference engine can perform deductive reasoning operations on them—*provided, however, that the programmer has fully anticipated precisely which rules and which facts will be required.* Missing facts can, however, be handled by directing a query to the user. In the preceding example, for instance, one could write the program so that were it found that Joe likes Mary, but no information was found indicating that Mary likes Joe, a query would be displayed on the screen to the user: "Does Mary like Joe?" If the user responds, "No," the program would deduce that the query ("Do Joe and Mary like each other?") is false. Using such techniques, then, a programmer can create a highly interactive program, one that allows the user to supply the program with situationally dependent information.

The rules contained in such programs need not all be of the true/false, either/or form indicated above. Most AI programming languages permit such rules to contain *confidence factors,* which assign a probability level to each rule. Confidence factors permit the programmer to express heuristic rules that contain qualifiers such as "probably" or "almost certainly." In the expert system shell VP-Planner, for instance, a rule could take the following form:

```
X likes Y IF (CONFIDENCE LEVEL 60%)
    X says X likes Y.
```

Expert systems created with these techniques have attracted no small attention in the commercial marketplace because of their ability to capture the practical, day-to-day expertise of highly skilled (and highly educated) human workers. An expert system is created by means of a process called *knowledge engineering,* in which a trained interviewer attempts to express an expert's knowledge as a set of computer-readable facts, rules, and situational queries. This process is more difficult than it might appear on first glance. An expert's knowledge does not consist merely of facts and rigid rules; it also includes heuristic rules of thumb that are acquired only after extensive experience (e.g., "It's usually best to start the melt cooling from well above the putative melting point," or "If a throat swab contains rod-shaped bacilli and it is suspected that the patient has diphtheria, then the rods are almost certainly diphtheria bacilli" [Collins, 1986: 12]). Such heuristics will not be found in textbooks; they are, in the main, "subjective, ill-codified, and partly judgmental" (Buchanan et al., 1983). Learned only through experience, they thus differ radically from the firm, fixed, and formalized rules that can be expressed in mathematical terms.

The point of knowledge engineering is to cull out the facts, the rules, and the heuristics that experts use, and to make them explicit enough that they can be expressed in a functioning computer program (Collins, 1986). The goal of this procedure is not to force inherently fuzzy knowledge into a highly formalized system, but to express it in a way that *captures* the best judgment of the expert, fuzzy and probabilistic as it may be. The goal is to conclude, in short, not that the rods *are* diphtheria bacilli, but that they are *almost certainly* diphtheria bacilli. To put it another way, knowledge engineering takes practical, experientially learned, fuzzy, and previously private knowledge and makes it *public* (Duda and Shortliffe, 1983: 265)—ultimately, so much so that it is accessible to nonexperts.

The achievement of expert system technology has let to an explosion of interest in expert system applications. Considerable controversy exists, however, about whether expert system technology will actually succeed in replacing human experts. At present, expert systems perform best within realms of expertise that involve microscopically specialized knowledge domains, such as classification (e.g., differential diagnosis in medicine) or process control (e.g., controlling a distillation stack in a chemical processing plant) (Duda and Shortliffe, 1983: 262; Feigenbaum and McCorduck, 1984: 91-92). The reason for success in these areas is hardly accidental. In both classification and process control, the expert system deals with a closed, restricted, and relatively unchanging domain of reality. It is far more difficult to devise expert systems to cope with domains of expertise in which expert knowledge—or the domain of reality with which it is concerned—makes use of common-sense knowledge or changes rapidly.

Common sense or tacit knowledge (Polanyi, 1967), as distinguished from the type of knowledge that is susceptible to representation in an expert system, is notoriously difficult to represent. Such knowledge permits a human being to *contextualize* a situation, that is, to determine whether it is appropriate, in one situation, to continue the sequence "2, 4, 6, 8" with "10, 12, 14, 16," and in another situation, with "Who do we appreciate?" (Collins, 1986: 13). *An expert system capable of using tacit knowledge of this type could perform such contextualizing operations only if it had been deliberately provided with the necessary information.* That is why the program engages the user in a "dialogue": When a situation arises that may have contingencies, the program asks for further (e.g., situation-dependent) meaning. It is indeed possible, to be sure, to create a program that queries the user (or otherwise supplies) such contextualizing information. Were a program asked to continue the sequence "2, 4, 6, 8," for example, it could query the user, "Is this a mathematical exercise or an adulation ritual?"

The central problem in the creation of expert systems, however, is that it is *exceptionally difficult to determine in advance* just what kinds of situational knowledge will be required to contextualize information properly:

> Suppose you are given a medical history that refers to a patient's weight as 14 pounds and age as 110 years. You would immediately suspect an error in the data, not because a person couldn't weigh 14 pounds or be 110 years old, but because the combination of the two is virtually impossible. In fact, you might suspect that the two entries had accidentally been reversed. An expert system designed to perform medical decision making would probably not catch this type of error unless it had been given tables of likely age/weight ratios to check against the data [Waterman, 1986: 12].

What is more, research on expert system development has disclosed a frustrating phenomenon: For every arithmetic increment in the system's breadth of expertise, there occurs an *exponential* increment in the number of situational contingencies *that must be foreseen for the program to operate effectively.* Such contingencies multiply exponentially at a ratio that is probably estimated conservatively to be 100 new contingencies for every 10% increase in the program's breadth of expertise. To obtain a 10% increase in performance in a medical diagnostic expert system, for instance, it was necessary to *quadruple* the number of rules (Waterman, 1986: 182). Summarizing these and other difficulties, Donald Waterman concludes: "If [common sense or general knowledge about the world] is crucial to solving a problem, the knowledge engineering approach will most likely fail" (Waterman, 1986: 182; Winograd, 1984).

It is for precisely this reason that some philosophers deny that expert systems contain knowledge, at least in the human sense. Susceptible to representation in an expert system is not knowledge in the sense that humans use it, but a pale imitation of such knowledge that has been whittled down to the point that its network of situational contingencies is manageable. The programmer, in short, creates a highly artificial micro world, and it is only in such micro worlds that AI techniques can function:

> The problem encountered in every attempt to move from micro-worlds to any aspect of the everyday world is that micro-worlds aren't worlds at all, or, from the other side, domains within the everyday world aren't anything like micro-worlds. This insight emerged in the attempt to program children's story understanding. It was soon discovered that the 'world' of even a single child's story, unlike a micro-world, is not a self-contained domain and cannot be treated independently of the larger everyday world onto which it opens. Everyday understanding is presupposed in every real domain, no matter how small. . . . Once this was realized, micro-world research and its successes were recognized for what they really were. . . [:] clever evasions of the real need to program . . . general competence and understanding [Searle, 1987].

According to Searle, then, genuine human knowledge "is not like a building which can be built up of tiny bricks—but is a whole somehow present in each of its parts." One could well term such knowledge *holographic*. A hologram is a laser-generated picture in which the whole picture is somehow interpenetrated in all of its parts, so that much (if not all) of the total picture can be generated from a fragment of the original. (There is some evidence, it should be noted, that human memory is holographic in this sense; even though there is some evidence of specific storage locations for specific memories, large brain lesions can occur without reducing memory retrieval capability.) The facts and rules one can put into an expert system are but pale imitations of this holographic knowledge. They have been whittled down into manageable form by stripping them, so far as possible, of situational contingencies and common-sense knowledge.

Even if one cannot accurately describe the rules of an expert system as "knowledge" in any human sense, is it not still possible to say that the expert system simulates human reasoning when it performs operations on these rules? It would seem, at least on first glance, that such operations do indeed resemble human reasoning. After all, the sine qua non of a true expert system is its ability to perform de novo reasoning operations on its rule base, thus deriving conclusions that are not explicitly stated anywhere in the rules but are nevertheless deducible from them. In reply to this frequently stated claim, however, it must be stressed that true de novo operations—deductions that are completely unforeseen by the programmer—are exceptionally rare in the actual performance of expert systems. The rarity of such deductions stems from the need, as just noted, for such systems to draw on contextual information (such as tables of likely age/weight ratios) whose relevance is exceptionally difficult to predict in advance; expert systems can function successfully, in fact, only when the breadth of the system is narrowed sufficiently that the situational contingencies are reduced down to a manageable level and they can all be built into the program.

What is more, it is demonstrable that expert systems perform their deductive operations in a form that differs radically from the techniques that humans apparently use. An expert system can answer a query only through a slow, sequential, and exhaustive search through the data base of facts and rules; every one of them must be examined before the deduction can be made. For this reason another upward limit appears on the breadth of expertise that such systems can handle; a program that requires more than 1,500 rules, for instance, will require a super fast minicomputer or mainframe to function at adequate levels of performance. People do not solve problems this way. We are always involved in some situation or context that seems to exclude most options and focuses our attention on the most likely avenues of problem solution (Dreyfus, 1987). Such contextual knowledge can indeed be supplied to the computer, to be sure, but only in minute quantities; formidable barriers appear when efforts to expand contextual knowledge are made.

Going further, Shanker (1987) argues that the expert system cannot be said in any intelligible sense to perform reasoning operations, since whatever reasoning is being simulated has been put there by the human programmer. As it processes the text-based rules by performing simple pattern-matching operations on them, the computer does not "understand" what it is doing; its understanding is zero (Dreyfus, 1987). In short, *it is the programmer's reasoning, not the computer's that one sees displayed on the screen* (Shanker, 1987). An expert system's "reasoning" capacity is little more, at best, than the reasoning of the knowledge engineer, and this reasoning stands or falls on the adequacy of the human process of knowledge extraction that occurs between the knowledge engineer and the human expert.

What we behold in expert systems, in short, is an exceptionally strong instance of the fetishizing of technology, in which the *social relations* that produce the technology are hidden and denied, coupled with an equally extraordinary attribution of understanding and intentionality to an artifact (Searle, 1987). Such ascriptions of intentionality to artifacts are common among AI researchers, one of whom made such an astonishing claim as, "Machines as simple as thermostats can be said to have beliefs, and having beliefs seems to be a characteristic of most machines capable of problem-solving performances." The argument may not be convincing for thermostats, but it is specious for expert systems—so much so, in fact, that an exceptionally tough-minded philosophical critique (see especially Shanker, 1987 and Dreyfus, 1987) is needed to dispel such attributions of intentionality and the misleading language with which they are expressed.

The inevitable conclusion of such a critique, in my view, is that expert systems do not contain knowledge; they contain limited numbers of text-based facts and rules. Expert systems do not simulate human expertise except in the narrowest sense; they can deal only with microscopically defined micro-worlds in which the number of situational contingencies is deliberately minimized and exhaustively searched. And expert systems do not perform "reasoning" operations; they use simple pattern-matching and other basic computer operations to follow deductive trails which are, for the most part, laid down in advance by the programmer. As will be seen next, it is absolutely essential that the mystifying veils surrounding such software be torn away before they are used in qualitative social research.

Expert Systems as Models of Everyday Cognition

The preunderstandings built into expert systems pose particular dangers to social scientists in that they suggest straightaway a particularly misleading research application of this software: its use to create psychologically valid models of cognition. An expert system, after all, appears to amount to a model of a human expert's cognitive processes. So why not use such software to create and explore models of folk or everyday cognition? The suggestion is by no means implicit. Charniak and McDermott (1985: 6) actually define artificial intelligence as "the study of [human] mental faculties through the use of computational models." Such assertions usually go hand-in-hand with what Shanker (1987) calls the Mechanist Thesis, namely, the claim that "the brain is a computer" or that "people think with programs." As will be seen, the claim that expert systems model human cognition is philosophically unintelligible and poses dangers for researchers who may find themselves seduced by it.

The fanfare surrounding the formal modeling of cognitive systems has died down considerably from its peaks in the mid-1960s, but expert system software will doubtless give it a new lease on life. In anthropology, for instance, much attention was devoted in the 1960s to ethnoscience. Ethnoscience sought to create models of the cultural knowledge a native actor needed to act in a way that would be judged normal and intelligible by natives themselves (e.g., Colby, 1966; Frake, 1962). Ethnoscience likened cultural knowledge to language—specifically, to a grammatical system, with its unitary, noncontradictory, and elegant network of rules. The purpose of ethnography was to discover the "grammar" of social behavior, and what is more, to put ethnography on a firm scientific footing. Ethnoscience would thus bring to ethnography all the advantages of formal models in mathematical sociology. Such advantages include "revealing gaps in knowledge, allowing for checks in incompleteness and redundancy, forcing knowledge to be represented explicitly, eliminating vagueness and ambiguity, and providing greater clarity and precision" (Brent, 1984: 256).

This enterprise proved disappointing, but expert system software may bring it back to life. Like other attempts to bring formal models to life in the qualitative study of social life, ethnoscience studies amounted to little more than the rigorous study of trivial, highly restricted problems with sophisticated techniques (Berreman, 1966; Keesing, 1966; Sweet, 1966). A major problem: Much cultural behavior does not appear to be as rigorously formulated as a language's grammar. That is precisely why expert system software is likely to fuel a new spate of attempts to create formal models of everyday cognitive systems. Expert system software, after all, is *expressly designed* to represent fuzzy, heuristic-based knowledge, and it would appear to be extremely well suited to the formal modeling of native thought. The problem with such notions, however, is that an expert system, no matter how well it simulates human expertise, can make no philosophically convincing claim (as already argued) to model or represent actual human cognitive processes.

One can carry this argument still further, as has Kobsa (1987). An AI program is not, in a strict sense, a *theory* about a cognitive structure, mechanism, or process; it is a computer version of all of these. And as any programmer will tell you, alternative algorithms exist for virtually all of the pattern matching, decision making, and other operations that take place in expert system programs. The choice of a particular algorithm over another is likely to be dictated, not by conformance to actual human psychological states, but to such matters as processing efficiency and effective use of computer memory. Even if one could claim that such systems actually processed knowledge in any sense akin to human knowledge, therefore, one would still have to agree with Kobsa (1987: 186) that "an AI model is merely one instantiation of some functional decomposition [of a problem], i.e., one member of a (perhaps infinite) set of mechanisms [algorithms] subsumable under this decomposition." In other words, every computer program (expert systems included) is only one of a set of possible solutions (i.e., algorithms) to the programming challenge, which is to produce the required output from a given input.

To repeat this point in another way, an algorithm is merely a procedural way of solving a problem by breaking it down into steps; *doing so, however, does not elucidate any properties of the real world.* Medieval clock makers, for instance, would never have been able to discover the Newtonian laws underlying their clocks' operation merely by building more and more sophisticated mechanisms (Weizenbaum, 1976). So an AI model, Kobsa concludes, is "a *model of a theory*. . . . this is completely different from a theory." It is therefore wrong to claim that an expert system can serve as a theory of cognition (which makes a claim to be psychologically valid). Such a system can, however, serve as a *model* of such a theory—and that is precisely why an expert system can prove of major value to qualitative research, as will be seen in the following section.

Expert Systems as a Tool for Discovery in the Field

Now that the preunderstandings built into expert system software have been unpacked, it is possible to discern precisely how such programs can contribute to qualitative research. And despite the negative tone of much that has been said in this chapter, I believe the promise is bright—so long as the software and its preunderstandings are clearly understood! The key, as Kobsa (1987: 187) stresses, is simple: "We should be careful not to be seduced into saying more than we justifiably can." What we can say is that expert systems provide the tools to create a *model of a theory of everyday cognition,* so long as we limit such analyses to microscopically defined realms of cultural knowledge.

What does it mean to create a "model of a theory"? A *theory* of cognition implies what Chomsky called psychological reality, namely, it makes an explicit claim to describe what actually happens inside someone's head. A *model of a theory,* however, makes no such claim. A model, by definition, shares only some of the attributes of the thing that it models; the researcher *knows* that the model does not possess all of the attributes of that which is modeled. Consider, for instance, a model mock-up of a new airliner in a wind tunnel: It possesses far less mass than the real thing, and lacks propulsion. Yet it will lift when winds are blown past it at high speed, and through cautious research the engineers can learn something about the aerodynamics of the prototype. Even though it does not possess all the attributes of its (real) prototype, a model compensates by offering *ease of manipulation.* By experimenting with the model, varying its attributes and manipulating its environment, one might be able to learn something about the behavior of the real thing. *Yet any such experiments must be predicated on a clear awareness that, no matter how apparently accurate the model might be, it is not the real thing.* Some of its attributes differ, perhaps radically, from that which it serves as an easily manipulated prototype, and such variations must always be kept in mind.

With all these caveats in plain view, then, one can argue that an expert system development language (such as PROLOG[7]) or shell (such as VP-Expert[8]) can provide exceptionally useful tools for qualitative research in the sense stressed throughout this book, namely, a hermeneutic spiral in which theoretical notions are constantly revised and refined through immersion in (and confrontation with) the data. Without making any claims that an expert system comprises a *theory* of everyday cognition, one can nevertheless use such a system to begin building a model of such a theory. The utility of such a model would lie not in any indefensible claim that it describes "how people actually think," but that it would be easily manipulated in a way that could prove fruitful in sessions with informants. The goal of such sessions would be, ideally, that the output of the system (regardless of its internal mechanisms, for which no claim to psychological reality would be made) would appear sensible to people familiar with the host culture.

An example should serve to illustrate the potential of this method, which (to the best of my knowledge) has never been attempted in the field. In my study of pilgrimage among the Tamil Hindus of northern Sri Lanka, I found that decisions about which pilgrimage site to visit were often guided by fuzzily formulated heuristics ("If a snake comes into your house, or you dream about a snake, you'd better make a vow to Nakapucanaiyamman, the goddess of the Nainativu shrine."). (An expression of such heuristics in VP-EXPERT rules follows) A research technique of profound value could, I believe, be built around the construction of an expert system that would capture such heuristics in consultation with native informants. As the model takes shape, its properties could be explored with informants, who can scrutinize the system's performance and point out when it performs at variance with native sensibilities. Once a coherent model has taken shape, it can be used to measure how well the model stands up in varying social contexts. Do Untouchables recognize this kind of reasoning? Do they dispute some of the rules? Do they use variant heuristics?

Expression of Folk Heuristics in VP-Expert Rules

10. X has *naka tosam* (confidence level 80%) IF:
     a snake has entered X's house OR
     X has dreamed about a snake.
11. X should make a vow to the goddess of Nainativu IF:
     X has *naka tosam* OR
     X desires a child

The goal of an investigation of this sort is not to create a theory of native cognition, but to create a model that *mediates* between native cognition and the researcher's culture, the audience to which his or her research report will be directed. (The implications of this point go beyond the goals of this book, but their general contours can be outlined here.) I don't believe for one minute that a Sri Lankan Tamil Hindu *thinks* in any way that could be described by such heuristics ("Aiyo! There's a snake in my house! Aiyo! I've been dreaming about snakes! I'd better make a vow to go to Nainativu if I don't get sick!"). What a person is *actually* thinking is a product of culture in interaction with history and biography (e.g., "When my aunt found a snake, she went to Nainativu," or "After I kill this damned thing, I'd better go to Nainativu, or the neighbors will talk"), furthermore, it is an expression of what Wittgenstein would call a mode of life, a way of behaving that becomes so much a part of everyday action that people never stop to think about it. The only validity such mediational models have is that they make cultural behavior moderately intelligible to outsiders, and when adequately expressed, they conform to the statements informants might make when pressed to talk about things they usually don't need to talk about (see, for further discussion, Cicourel, 1973; Douglas, 1976; Johnson, 1975; Manning, 1979).

It is in precisely this sense that the chief shortcoming of expert system software, namely, the falsity of the claim that its rules actually express psychologically valid knowledge, turns out to have an advantage. *An expert system's rules are precisely the kinds of mediational models that ethnographers strive to formulate.* If they correspond to anything at all in the expert's way of thinking, Dreyfus (1987) argues, it is more to the nervous formulations of an earnest but inept novice than to the artless (and wordless) assurance of a seasoned professional. Such formulations do not really have the rich contextual linkages to the rest of a huge, complex, and ultimately ineluctable world of folk experience, a world that can be appreciated only by long years of immersion. But they contain enough of this culturally provided information to put the indigenous point of view within the researcher's grasp, as they do for novices, in that they allow the researcher to explore with informants the gross contours (at least) of social action and its implications. To put it another way, Agar (1986) argues that all ethnographic models attempt to translate between one tradition (the informants') and another (the researchers'). All expert systems are mediational in precisely this way, although their mediational role is hidden (and actively denied): They seek to mediate between the cognitive system of a human expert and the requirements of today's primitive computer hardware. The tools, in short, are precisely honed for the job.

When used in a recursive, hermeneutic spiral of creation, confrontation, and revision, in sum, an expert system can provide precisely the tools a researcher needs to formulate a mediational expression of this sort and explore its properties thoroughly—so long as the knowledge domain under investigation is relatively limited. No one really knows, as yet, whether the number of rules needed to model the decisions police make, for instance, exceeds the number of rules a physician uses to diagnose diseases of the blood, but intuition suggests that the numbers are comparable.

The point of using an expert system in qualitative research settings, reiterating a point made at the conclusion of the previous chapter (and indeed, throughout this book), is not to create a computer program that is an *end* in itself; on the contrary, it is to harness microcomputer hardware and software so that it serves as a *means* to enhanced awareness, theoretical sensitivity, and humanistic understanding. Such tools can come into their own in qualitative research, as I hope this book has demonstrated, only when a thorough attempt is made to see them as they are. Like language, technology is our creation, and we imbue it with a symbolism whose potency we are only now beginning to guess. As Lescek Kolakowski says, man can dig no well deep enough that, at the bottom, he cannot see his face.

NOTES

1. FYI, Inc.: O. Box 26481, Austin, TX 78755.

2. Electronic Text Corporation, 5600 North University Ave., Provo, UT 84604.

3. Guide, Owl International, Inc., 14218 N.E. 21st Ave., Bellevue, WA 98007.

4. Pro Tem Software, 814 Tolman Dr., Stanford, CA 94305.

5. TEXTPACK V (MS-DOS version) (ZUMA, Postfach 5969, D-6800 Mannheim 1, West Germany); Micro-OCP (Oxford University Press, Walton Street, Oxford, OX2 GDP, U.K.); WordCruncher (Electronic Text Corporation, 5600 North University Ave., Provo, UT 84604).

6. A note of caution: not all idea processing programs have the text-storage, memory-resident, and text-moving features required for this exceptionally fruitful analytic strategy. At this writing, the best available program for this purpose is PC-OUTLINE, available on a shareware basis from local computer bulletin boards or from PC-SIG (1030-D East Duane Avenue, Sunnyvale, CA 94086).

7. A good microcomputer implementation of PROLOG is TURBO PROLOG (Borland International, 4585 Scotts Valley Drive, Scotts Valley, CA 95066). An educational PROLOG is available on a shareware basis from Automata Design Associates, 1570 Arran Way, Dresher, PA 19025. The standard introduction to PROLOG programming is Clocksin and Mellish (1984).

8. Paperback Software, 2830 Ninth Street, Berkeley, CA 94710.

REFERENCES

ADAMS, A. L. (1979) "Planning search strategies for maximum retrieval from bibliographic databases." Online Review 3.

AGAR, M. (1983) "Microcomputers as field tools." Computers in the Humanities 17: 19-26.

AGAR, M. (1986) Speaking of Ethnography. (Sage University Paper, Qualitative Research Methods series, Vol. 2) Beverly Hills, CA: Sage.

ALTHEIDE, D. L. (1985) "Keyboarding as a social form." Computers and the Social Sciences 3.

ALTHEIDE, D. L. (1987) "Ethnographic content analysis." Qualitative Sociology 10: 65-77.

ALTHEIDE, D. L. and R. P. SNOW (1979) Media Logic. Beverly Hills, CA: Sage.

ARIES, E. (1977) "Male-female interpersonal styles in all male, all female, and mixed groups," pp. 292-299 in A. G. Sargent (ed.) Beyond Sex Roles. New York: West.

ARNOLD, D. O. (1982) "Qualitative field methods," in R. B. Smith and P. K. Manning (eds.) Qualitative Methods (Vol. II of Handbook of Social Science Methods). Cambridge, MA: Ballanger.

BARKER, J. and H. DOWNING (1985) "Word processing and the transformation of patriarchal relations of control in the office," pp. 147-169 in D. MacKenzie and J. Wajcman (eds.) The Social Shaping of Technology. Philadelphia: Open University Press.

BARR, A. and E. A. FEIGENBAUM (1981) The Handbook of Artificial Intelligence, Vol. 1. Stanford: Stanford University Press.

BECKER, H. S. and B. GEER (1960) "Participant observation: the analysis of qualitative field data," pp. 267-289 in R. N. Adams and J. J. Priess (eds.) Human Organization Research: Field Relations and Techniques. Homewood, IL: Dorsey.

BECKER, H. W., A. C. GORDON, and R. K. LEBAILLY (1984) "Field work with the computer: criteria for assessing systems." Qualitative Sociology 7: 16-33.

BERREMAN, G. (1966) "Anemic and emetic analyses in social anthropology." American Anthropologist 68: 346-354.

BERNSTEIN, J. (1981) The Analytical Engine. New York: William Morrow.

BLAXTER, M. (1979) "Symposium on the handling of qualitative data." Sociological Review 27.

BOLTER, J. (1984) Turing's Man: Western Culture in the Computer Age. Chapel Hill: University of North Carolina Press.

BRENT, E. (1984) "Qualitative computing: approaches and issues." Qualitative Sociology 7: 34-60.

BUCHANAN, B., D. BARSTOW, R. BECHTEL, J. BENNETT, W. CLANCY, C. LULIKOWSKI, T. MITCHELL, and D. A. WATERMAN (1983) "Constructing an expert system," pp. 127-167 in F. Hayes-Roth, D. A. Waterman, and D. B. Lenat (eds.) Building Expert Systems. Reading, MA: Addison-Wesley.

BUCHANAN, R. A. (1965) Technology and Social Progress. Oxford: Pergamon.

BUNNELL, D. (1987) "The participatory PC." PC World ((December): 15-32.

BURTON, D. M. (1980) "Automated concordances and word indexes: the fifties." Computers and the Humanities 15: 1-14.

BURTON, D. M. (1981a) "Automated concordances and word indexes: the early sixties and the early centers." Computers and the Humanities 15: 83-100.

BURTON, D. M. (1981b) "Automated concordances and word indexes: the process, the programs, and the products." Computers and the Humanities 15: 139-154.

BURTON, D. M. (1982) "Automated concordances and word indexes: machine decisions and editorial revisions." Computers and the Humanities 16: 195-218.

BUSH, V. (1945) "As we may think." Atlantic Monthly 176 (February 1945): 45-54.

CHARMAZ, K. (1983) The grounded theory approach: an explication and interpretation, pp. 109-126 in R. M. Emerson (ed.) Contemporary Field Research: A Collection of Readings. Boston: Little Brown.

CHARNIAK, E. and D. V. McDERMOTT (1985) Introduction to Artificial Intelligence. Reading, MA: Addison-Wesley.

CHOMKSY, N. (1959) "Review of B. F. Skinner, verbal behavior." Language 35: 26-58.

CICOUREL, A. (1973) Cognitive Sociology. Harmondsworth, England: Penguin.

CLOCKSIN, W. F. and C. S. MELLISH (1984) Programming in Prolog (2nd ed.). New York: Springer-Verlag.

COCKBURN, C. (1985) "The material of male power," pp. 165- 172 in D. MacKenzie and J. Wajcman (eds.) The Social Shaping of Technology. Philadelphia: Open University Press.

COLBY, B. N. (1966) "Ethnographic semantics: a preliminary survey." Current Anthropology 7: 3-32.

COLLIER, R. M. 1983. "The word processor and revision strategies." College Composition and Communication 34: 149-155.

COLLINS, H. (1986) "Expert systems and the science of knowledge," in W. B. Bijker, T. P. Hughes, and T. J. Pinch (eds.) The Social Construction of Technological Systems: New Directions in the Sociology and History of Technology. Cambridge, MA: MIT Press.

COLLINS, H. and T. PINCH (1979) "The construction of the paranormal: nothing unscientific is happening," pp. 237-270 in R. Wallis (ed.) On the Margins of Science: The Social Construction of Rejected Knowledge. Keele: University of Keele.

COLLINS, T. W. (1982) "Social science research and the microcomputer." Sociological Methods and Research 9: 438-460.

CONRAD, P. and S. REINHARZ (1984) "Computers and qualitative data." Qualitative Sociology 7: 3-15.

DOUGLAS, J. D. (1976) Investigative Social Research. Beverly Hills, CA: Sage.

DREYFUS, H. L. (1987) "Misrepresenting human intelligence," pp. 41-54 in R. P. Born and I. B. Born-Lechleitner (eds.) Artificial Intelligence. London: Croom-Helm.

DUDA, R. O. and E. H. SHORTLIFFE (1983) "Expert systems research." Science 220 (4594): 261-268.

DUNPHY, D. C. (1966) "The construction of categories for content analysis dictionaries," pp. 134-168 in P. J. Stone et al. (eds.) The General Inquirer. Cambridge: MIT Press.

ELLUL, J. (1962) "The technological order." Technology and Culture 3: 394-421.

FEIGENBAUM, E. A. and P. McCORDUCK (1984) The Fifth Generation: Artificial Intelligence and Japan's Challenge to the World. New York: Signet.

FELDMAN, P. R. and B. NORMAN (1987) The Wordworthy Computer: Classroom and Research Applications in Language and Literature. New York: Knopf.

FIELDING, N. and J. FIELDING (1986) Linking Data. (Sage University Paper, Qualitative Research Methods series, No. 4.) Beverly Hills, CA: Sage.

FLOWER, L. and J. R. HAYES (1980) "The cognition of discovery: defining a rhetorical problem." College Composition and Communication 31: 21-32.

FLOWER, L. and J. R. HAYES (1981) "A cognitive process theory of writing." College Composition and Communication 32: 365-387.

FRAKE, C. (1962) "The ethnographic study of cognitive systems," pp. 72-85 in Gladwin and W. G. Sturtevant (eds.) Anthropology and Human Behavior. Washington: Anthropological Society of Washington.

FREIDHEIM, E. A. (1984) "Field research and word processor files: a technical note." Qualitative Sociology 7: 90-97.

GERSON, E. (1987) "Another way of working with text." Qualitative Sociology 10: 204-207.

GILBERT, G. N. and C. HEATH (1986) "Text, competence, and logic: an exercise." Qualitative Sociology 9: 215-237.

GILLESPIE, G. W. (1984) "Using word processor macros for computer-assisted qualitative analysis." Qualitative Sociology 9: 283-292.

GLASER, B. G. (1978) Theoretical Sensitivity: advances in the methodology of grounded theory. Mill Valley, CA: Sociology Press..

GLASER, B. G. and A. L. STRAUSS (1967) The Discovery of Grounded Theory: Strategies for Qualitative Research. New York: Aldine.

GODELIER, M. (1972) Rationality and Irrationality in Economics. New York: Monthly Review Press.

GOLDSCHMIDT, W. (1972) "An ethnography of encounters: a methodology for the enquiry into the relation between the individual and society." Current Anthropology 13: 59-78.

GOONATILAKE, S. (1984) Aborted Discovery: Science and Creativity in the Third World. London: Zed.

HALLIDAY, M. and R. HASAN (1976) Cohesion in English. London: Longman.

HAYES-ROTH, F., D. A. WATERMAN, and D. LENAT [eds.] (1983) Building Expert Systems. Reading, MA: Addison-Wesley.

HOCKEY, S. (1980) A Guide to Computer Applications in the Humanities. Baltimore: Johns Hopkins University Press.

HOLSTI, O. (1969) Content Analysis for the Social Sciences and Humanities. Reading, MA: Addison-Wesley.

HOLTON, G. (1973) Thematic Origins of Scientific Thought: Kepler to Einstein. Cambridge: Harvard University Press.

JOHNSON, D. B. (1979) National Party Platforms, 1840-1976. Urbana: University of Illinois Press.

JOHNSON, J. (1975) Doing Fieldwork. New York: Free Press.

KEESING, R. M. (1966) "Comment on B. N. Colby (1966)." Current Anthropology 7: 23.

KELLY, E. F. and P. J. STONE (1975) Computer Recognition of English Word Senses. Amsterdam: North Holland.

KENNY, A. (1982) The Computation of Style: An Introduction to Statistics for Students of Literature and the Humanities. Oxford: Pergamon.

KIRK, J. and M. MILLER (1986) Reliability and Validity in Qualitative Research (Sage

84

University Paper, Qualitative Research Methods series, Vol. 1). Beverly Hills, CA: Sage.

KLINGEMANN, H., P. P. MOHLER, and R. P. WEBER (1982) "Cultural indicators based on content analysis." Quality and Quantity 16: 1-18.

KOBSA, A. (1987) "What is explained by AI Models," pp. 174-189 in R. P. Born and I. B. Born-Lechleitner (eds.) Artificial Intelligence. London: Croom-Helm.

KRIPPENDORF, K. (1980) Content Analysis: An Introduction to Its Methodology. Beverly Hills, CA: Sage.

LASSWELL, H. D. (1965) "Why be quantitative?," in H. D. Lasswell et al. (eds.) Language of Politics. Cambridge: MIT Press.

LASSWELL, H. D. and J. Z. NAMENWIRTH (1968) The Lasswell Value Dictionary. New Haven: Yale University.

LAYTON, E. (1974) "Technology as knowledge." Technology and Culture 15: 31-414.

LEVIN, M. L. (1986) Technological Determinism in Social Data Analysis. Computers and the Social Sciences 2: 201-207.

LINDKVIST, K. (1981) "Approaches to textual analysis," pp. 23-42 in K. E. Rosengren (ed.) Advances in Content Analysis. Beverly Hills, CA: Sage.

LYMAN, P. (1984) "Reading, writing, and word processing: toward a phenomenology of the computer age." Qualitative Sociology 7: 75-89.

MACKENZIE, D. and J. WAJCMAN [eds.] (1985) "Introduction," pp. 1-25 in The Social Shaping of Technology. Philadelphia: Open University.

MANNING, P. K. (1979) "Metaphors of the field: varieties of organizational discourse." Administrative Science Quarterly 24: 660-671.

MANNING, P. K. (1982) "Analytic induction," pp. 273-302 in Robert B. Smith and P. K. Manning (eds.) Qualitative Methods (Vol. II of Handbook of Social Science Methods). Cambridge, MA: Ballinger.

MERTON, R. K. (1968) Social Theory and Social Structure. New York: Free Press.

MILES, M. (1979) "Qualitative data as an attractive nuisance: the problem of analysis." Administrative Science Quarterly 24: 590-601.

MOSTELLER, F. and D. L. WALLACE (1964) Inference and Disputed Authorship: The Federalist. Reading, MA: Addison-Wesley.

MULKAY, M. (1979) Science and the Sociology of Knowledge. London: Allen and Unwin.

NAMENWIRTH, J. Z. (1969a) "Marks of distinction: a content analysis of British mass and prestige editorials." American Journal of Sociology 74: 343-360.

NAMENWIRTH, J. Z. (1969b) "Some long and short term trends in American political value," in G. Gerbner et al. (eds.) The Analysis of Communication Content. New York: John Wiley.

NAMENWIRTH, J. Z. (1970) "Prestige newspapers and the assessment of elite opinions." Journalism Quarterly 47: 318-323.

NAMENWIRTH, J. Z. (1973) "The wheels of time and the interdependence of value change." Journal of Interdisciplinary History 3: 649-683.

NAMENWIRTH, J. Z. (1983) "Why cultural indicators?" in G. Melischeck, K. E. Rosengren, and J. Stappers (eds.) Cultural Indicators. Vienna: Austrian Academy of Sciences.

NAMENWIRTH, J. Z. and H. D. LASWELL (1970) The Changing Language of American Values: A Computer Study of Selected Party Platforms. Beverly Hills, CA: Sage.

NELSON, T. H. (1974) Computer Lib. Chicago: Hugo's Book Service.

NELSON, T. H. (1980) "Replacing the printed word: a complete literary system," pp. 1013-1023 in S. H. Lavington (ed.) Information Processing 80. New York: North-Holland.

NOBLE, D. (1986) Forces of Production: A Social History of Industrial Automation. New York: Oxford University Press.

OAKMAN, R. (1984) Computer Methods for Literary Research (2nd ed.). Athens: University of Georgia Press.

O'LEARY, T. and B. WILLIAMS (1986) Computers and Information Processing. Menlo Park, CA: Benjamin/Cummins.

PACEY, A. (1983) The Culture of Technology. Cambridge, MA: MIT Press.

PFAFFENBERGER, B. (1979) "The Kataragama pilgrimage: Hindu-Buddhist interaction and its significance in Sri Lanka's polyethnic social system." Journal of Asian Studies 38: 253-270.

PFAFFENBERGER, B. (1980) "Social communication in Dravidian ritual." Journal of Anthropological Research 36: 196-219.

PFAFFENBERGER, B. (1981) "The cultural dimension of Tamil separatism in Sri Lanka." Asian Survey 21: 196-219.

PFAFFENBERGER, B. (1982) Caste in Tamil Culture: The Religious Foundations of Sudra Domination in Tamil Sri Lanka (South Asia Series No. 7). Syracuse: Maxwell School of Foreign and Comparative Studies.

PFAFFENBERGER, B. (1983) "Serious pilgrims and frivolous tourists: the chimera of tourism in the pilgrimages of Sri Lanka." Annals of Tourism Research 10: 57-84.

PFAFFENBERGER, B. (1987) "Word processing and text revision: interpreting the empirical evidence." Computers and Composition Journal 1: 105-118.

PFAFFENBERGER, B. (1987a) Personal Computer Applications: A Strategy for the Information Society. Boston: Little-Brown.

PFAFFENBERGER, B. (forthcoming-a) "Fetishized objects and humanized nature: toward an anthropology of technology." Man.

PFAFFENBERGER, B. (forthcoming-b) End-User Searching: The Nature and Prospects of a New Information Technology. Boston: G. K. Hall.

PINCH, T. and W. BIJKER (1984) "The social construction of facts and artifacts: or how the sociology of science and the sociology of technology might benefit each other." Social Studies of Science 14: 399-441.

PINCH, T., W. BIJKER and T. HUGHES (1987) The Social Construction of Technological Systems: New Directions in the Sociology and History of Technology. Cambridge: MIT Press.

PODOLEFSKY, A. and C. McCARTY (1983) "Topical sorting: a technique for computer-assisted qualitative data analysis." American Anthropologist 85: 886-890.

POLANYI, M. (1967) The Tacit Dimension. New York: Anchor.

POOL, I. (1952) Symbols of Democracy. Stanford: Stanford University Press.

PRESTON, M. J. and S. S. COLEMAN (1978) "Some considerations concerning encoding and concording texts." Computers and the Humanities 12: 3-12.

ROHMAN, D. G. (1965) "Pre-writing: the stage of discovery in the writing process." College Composition and Communication 16: 106-112.

ROSENGREN, K. E. (1981) Advances in Content Analysis. Beverly Hills, CA: Sage.

SCHOLTE, B. (1974) "Toward a reflexive and critical anthropology," pp. 430-457 in D. Hymes (ed.) Reinventing Anthropology. New York: Random House.

SCHUTZ, A. (1967) The Problem of Social Reality (Vol. I. of Collected Papers, M. Natanson, ed.). The Hague: Martinus Nijhoff.

SEARLE, J. R. (1987) "Minds, brains, and programs," pp. 18-40 in R. P. Born and I. B. Born-Lechleitner (eds.) Artificial Intelligence. London: Croom-Helm.

SEIDEL, J. V. and J. A. CLARK (1984) "The ETHNOGRAPH: a computer program for the analysis of qualitative data." Qualitative Sociology 7: 110-125.

SHANKER, S. G. (1987) "The decline and fall of the mechanist metaphor," pp. 72-131 in R. P. Born and I. B. Born-Lechleitner (eds.) Artificial Intelligence. London: Croom-Helm.

SHELLY, A. and E. SIBERT (1986) "Using logic programming to facilitate qualitative data analysis." Qualitative Sociology 9: 145-161.

SMITH, R. B. and P. K. MANNING (1982) "Preface," pp. xvii-xx in R. B. Smith and P. K. Manning (eds.) Qualitative Methods (Vol. II of Handbook of Social Science Methods). Cambridge: Ballinger.

SPRADLEY, J. P. (1979) The Ethnographic Interview. New York: Holt, Rinehart and Winston.

SPROULL, L. S. and R. F. SPROULL (1982) "Managing and analyzing behavioral records: explorations in nonnumeric data analysis." Human Organization 41: 283-290.

STONE, P. J., D. C. DUNPHY, M. S. SMITH, and D. M. OGILVIE (1966) The General Inquirer: A Computer Approach to Content Analysis. Cambridge: MIT Press.

SWEET, L. (1966) "Comment on 'Ethnographic Semantics' by B. N. Colby." Current Anthropology 7: 24-25.

SYKES, R. E. (1977) "Techniques of data collection and reduction in systematic field observation." Behavior Research Methods and Instrumentation 9: 407-417.

TURKLE, S. (1984) The Second Self: Computers and the Human Spirit. New York: Simon and Schuster.

TURNBULL, C. (1962) The Forest People. New York: Simon & Schuster.

WALKER, A. W. (1975) The Empirical Delineation of Two Musical Taste Cultures: A Content Analysis of Best-Selling Soul and Popular Recordings from 1962-1973. Ph.D. dissertation, New School for Social Research.

WATERMAN, D. A. (1986) A Guide to Expert Systems. Reading, MA: Addison-Wesley.

WEBER, R. P. (1983) "Content analytic cultural indicators," in G. Melischek, K. E. Rosengren, and J. Stappers (eds.) Cultural Indicators. Vienna: Austrian Academy of Sciences.

WEBER, R. P. (1984) "Computer-generated content analysis: a short primer." Qualitative Sociology 7: 126-174.

WEIZENBAUM, J. (1976) Computer Power and Human Reason. San Francisco: W. H. Freeman.

WHITE, L. (1959) The Evolution of Culture. New York: McGraw-Hill.

WILLIAMSON, M. (1987) "At DuPont, expert systems are key to AI implementation." PC Week (January 13): 35, 57.

WINKLER, K. J. (1985) "Questioning the science in social science, scholars signal a 'turn to interpretation'." Chronicle of Higher Education (June 26, 1985): 5.

WINNER, L. (1986) The Whale and the Reactor. Chicago: University of Chicago Press.

WINOGRAD, T. (1984) "Computer software for working with language." Scientific American 251 (February 4): 130-145)

ZYLAB CORPORATION (1985) "Anthropologists dig for data with ZyIndex." Press release.

ABOUT THE AUTHOR

BRYAN PFAFFENBERGER, a Phi Beta Kappa graduate of University of California, Berkeley (1971), received his M.A. (1972) and Ph.D. (1977) degrees in anthropology from the same institution. He taught until 1985 at Knox College, a small and selective liberal arts institution in Illinois, where he was Assistant and then Associate Professor (with tenure) of Anthropology. Since 1985, he has taught at the University of Virginia, where he is Assistant Professor of Humanities and Associate Director, Center for South Asian Studies. He has done ethnographic fieldwork in Sri Lanka (1973, 1974-1975, 1982, and 1988) and Mexico (1978 and 1982-1983), and contributed numerous articles and a book to the anthropological literature. His research interests include the anthropological study of technological innovation and technology transfer, the social history of Third World industrialization, and the sociology of ethnic conflict in Sri Lanka.

NOTES